Jeff Park

writing at the edge

Narrative and Writing Process Theory

PETER LANG
New York • Washington, D.C./Baltimore • Bern
Frankfurt am Main • Berlin • Brussels • Vienna • Oxford

Library of Congress Cataloging-in-Publication Data
Park, Jeff.
Writing at the edge: narrative and writing process theory / Jeff Park.
p. cm. — (Counterpoints: studies in the postmodern theory of education; v. 248)
Includes bibliographical references.
1. English language—Rhetoric—Study and teaching.
2. Report writing—Study and teaching (Higher) . 3. Narration (Rhetoric).
I. Title. II. Series: Counterpoints (New York, N.Y.); v. 248.
PE1404.P365   808'.042'071'1—dc22   2004022836
ISBN 0-8204-6785-5
ISSN 1058-1634

Bibliographic information published by **Die Deutsche Bibliothek**.
Die Deutsche Bibliothek lists this publication in the "Deutsche
Nationalbibliografie"; detailed bibliographic data is available
on the Internet at http://dnb.ddb.de/.

Cover design by Lisa Barfield
Cover art by David Alexander, *Trails, high octane river reflects*,
78 × 104 (inches), acrylic on canvas, 2002–2003

The paper in this book meets the guidelines for permanence and durability
of the Committee on Production Guidelines for Book Longevity
of the Council of Library Resources.

© 2005 Peter Lang Publishing, Inc., New York
275 Seventh Avenue, 28th Floor, New York, NY 10001
www.peterlangusa.com

All rights reserved.
Reprint or reproduction, even partially, in all forms such as microfilm,
xerography, microfiche, microcard, and offset strictly prohibited.

Printed in the United States of America

Acknowledgments

I dedicate this book to my parents. My father, James Park, died just before I began the book, and my mother, Carol Park, died soon after I completed the first draft of the manuscript. Their love and presence infuse and surround this work.

I also want to acknowledge the honor, courage and wisdom of all the writers who have attended our Writers' Group sessions over the last ten years. In their humility and compassion, I have learned much about life and myself. My gratitude goes far beyond words.

I especially want to express deep thanks to the four members of the Writers' Group who shared their ideas on writing for this book—Brian Borley, Albert Chatsis, "Warren McDonald," and "Caroline Murphy"—all important discourse and writing theorists.

I want to thank Sam Robinson for his constant support, wisdom, insight and kindness. Sam was actively involved with the Writers' Group for several years, and remains instrumental in the publishing and editing of the annual books of compiled writings.

Finally, I want to thank David Alexander for allowing me to use his painting for the book. When I first conceptualized the cover design, I wanted to have it reflect the thematic and metaphoric content of the text. David's painting of a landscape reflected in a river is a strong objective correlative for the metaphor of the riparian zone.

Contents

PRELUDE: ENTERING THE SITE / SIGHT 1

PART I: INTO THE RIVER 5

    Chapter One: The Writers' Group 7
    Chapter Two: Writing Theory and the Shift to Process 15
    Chapter Three: Narrative as Knowing, Evocation, and Being 37

PART II: THE RIPARIAN ZONE 49

    Chapter Four: Narratives as Integrated Research 51

PART III: INTO THE WORLD 99

    Chapter Five: At the Edge of Writing and Writing Theory 101
    Chapter Six: The Writing of the Participants 107
    Chapter Seven: Revisiting Writing Process Theory 133
    Chapter Eight: Pedagogy of the Riparian Zone 153

CODA 165

REFERENCES 169

Prelude

Entering the Site/Sight

I'm standing at the edge of the doorway to a living room crowded with over twenty members of the Writers' Group that I have been involved with for over ten years. All the writers are members of a mental health organization, and have all been labeled as being mentally ill at some point in their lives.

Each year Sam Robinson and I publish a self-funded book of all the writing that has been done at the Writers' Group. We compile, type, organize, and edit the collected writings of the group, and then bind the finished product into a book format. The writing group participants are responsible for naming the book. They suggest possible titles, and I collect their choices and conduct a vote. Over the years the book titles suggest a certain narrative direction, reflecting a progression of confidence within the group:

1993	*Solitudes*
1994	*Beyond Solitude*
1995	*Just As We Are*
1996	*Revealing the Inner Self*
1997	*When Words Take Wings*
1998	*Our Words, Ourselves*
1999	*Reaching for Infinity*
2000	*Flashing Thoughts, Whispering Words*
2001	*Write From the Heart*
2002	*New Lives, New Words*
2003	*Restless Words*
2004	*Write to Survive*

These titles suggest a movement in perspective–from people seeing themselves as isolated individuals to writers meaningfully connected to others and the rest of the world. Somehow, the writing that is completed each week adds to a growing sense of confidence, social belonging, and caring for others.

I have a stack of this year's book of collected writings on a small table beside me in the hallway. The writers are talking nervously to each other, anxiously waiting to see their words in print. At the end of the year, Sam and I invite all the writers who have participated during the year to a barbecue as a celebration of the year's accomplishments. After the barbecue, we hand out the books. We used to think that the dinner was the highlight of the year. We were wrong. It is the handing out of the year-end book that is the high-water mark.

In the living room, the writers are getting restless, waiting to receive this year's book, and then sign the copies of the other members. This year before I hand out the books, I ask if anyone wants to say anything. A few members say brief words, mostly thanking Sam and me for organizing the writing sessions and the year-end barbecue. Brian Borley, one of the four major participants in this book, tells the rest of the group how important writing is to him, and how much he looks forward to the weekly sessions. He says that writing is his playground and that he loves to play with language. He says that writing is one of the most important activities in his life. Fiona thanks all of us for just accepting her the way she is. She says that she doesn't mind taking the bus for over an hour to get to the meetings because the Writers' Group is one of the highlights of her week.

But it is Albert Chatsis who really surprises me when he speaks with raw honesty and candor. Albert usually has a half-smile on his face, and his eyes constantly read the room, gauging reactions and responses as he speaks slowly, often with long pauses. Albert, another major participant in this book, is always laughing, and likes to remind all of us that he was the first member of the Writers' Group. This time when he speaks he is very serious. From his chair Albert says, "I used to be an angry man. I was angry at white people, the police, and the justice system. I was mad at women because my wife had just left me for another man. I was mad at the whole world. Because of the Writers' Group, I have changed. I told my stories here. People listened to me and accepted me for who I am. I like to write about Native things, about the old ways. I am not an angry person anymore. I am a creative person now, and it is all because of the Writers' Group."

How can writing, and belonging to a writing group, transform someone who doesn't believe in anything except loss and injustice and pain and betrayal into a person who has pride in himself and his accomplishments? Maybe writing is

Entering the Site/Sight

more than an activity to communicate ideas to others. Maybe writing, by acting as a site of self-construction, is one of the dominant ways people in the modern world create a sense of who they are, and how they relate to others. Maybe it is time to reconsider the value of writing and what it means to write.

For this book, I use narrative inquiry as a dominant methodology and a way of knowing, as well as a way of being in the world. The narratives created for this book are central to an understanding of the act of writing. It is common for writing theorists and educators to use narrative to support pedagogical theory based on praxis. I have reversed the concept in many ways. I wanted the narratives, as evocations of the writers, to be the heart of the book. I have consequently placed the section called "Narrative as Integrated Research," which includes four narratives of individual writers, in the middle of the book. I believe that these writers, who have often been dismissed as marginalized "consumers," are central to the understanding of writing. In many ways, I consider their ideas on writing and the importance of the act of writing to be as valuable as those of many noted discourse theorists. The writers and their stories are the heart of this book, *Writing at the Edge: Narrative and Writing Process Theory*.

Part I

Into the River

"Every authorized system renders the truth of the marginalized invisible; reclaiming those truths demands a dedicated energy of subversion."

Dennis Lee,
from "Body Music: Notes on Rythmic Poetry"

Chapter One

The Writers' Group

Writing at the Edge explores the experiences and writing of four members of the Writers' Group that is associated with the Canadian Mental Health Association (CMHA) in a midwestern city in Canada. In this book, I consider the value and importance individual writers ascribe to the act of writing, both as an individual activity and as a meaningful social activity. I look at how people write, and why they write, exploring both autonomy and community within the discourse community of the Writers' Group. No one writes in complete isolation, and issues of race, gender, power and politics are always relevant forces that deeply affect writers and their writing. The Writers' Group is a community of writers completely removed from typical educational or vocational contexts. The writers don't have to write for their jobs, or for educational success, but instead write for enjoyment and a sense of discovering the world, and to gain an understanding of who they are.

I focus on the value of personal writing, or what James Britton (1970, 1972, 1979, 1980) classified as "expressive writing"—a type of writing that he claimed was "close to the self" (Britton, 1972, p. 96). I extend Britton's concept of expressive writing, and his idea of self to suggest that individual writers exist in a paradoxical space of being both autonomous selves containing multiplicities and contradictions, and social and cultural constructions.

I reconsider what writing "close to the self" means by reexamining early writing-process theory, and by questioning assumptions of what constitutes a "self." White and Hellerich (1998) define the postmodern individual as "both a single persona and a multiple of selves functioning in various social and cultural capacities" (p. 11). I use the term "self" as a unifying term, with the understanding that the self is both a multiplicity and a singular entity. It is within this paradoxical space that the individual is created, and that meaning of self is always within larger social and cultural frameworks.

In reexamining the value of personal, or expressive, writing I use the metaphor of the riparian zone for several reasons. In ecology, a riparian zone borders a river, stream or lake, and acts as a transition zone between upland and aquatic ecosystems. Riparian zones are among the most diverse biological systems in the world, although they comprise a very small proportion of landmass. To consider this metaphor, I suggest that expressive writing is the place where self and culture meet—a place that is both a zone of construction of the self, and a site of negotiation of meaning between the personal and the social. Writing is both an individual act and a social construction, influenced by membership within a number of discourse communities. It is within that diverse space that meaning is created. In this book, I propose that writers create all writing, however personal, in a metaphoric space of great diversity—a riparian zone—between an individual writer and others. In this space, the writer constructs a sense of self, and then negotiates relationships with others and the world through the creation of the written texts, which act as cultural artifacts. Writing in the expressive function is writing at the edge of self and the world.

This book is not intended as a history of writing-process or composition theory; in fact, it is quite discursive of such valuable theoretical lenses as discourse theory, critical theory, and cultural theory. Writing theory is extremely complex and varied. One of the major shifts has been from a product-based approach to a process-based approach. Writing theorists and educational practitioners require more knowledge about the nature of writing, and the way it is being taught in classrooms, than they used to. Teachers often attach values and teaching practices that were effective under the product-based paradigm to the new writing-process paradigm without considering the differences. What is now needed is to explore in greater depth, and to define more carefully, the new writing paradigm. I believe it is time to revisit writing-process theory, and to extend the purposes and practices of this theory to include self-development and personal growth within complex social and cultural contexts.

The focus for this book is on personal writing, or expressive writing. A second focus is on freewriting, because it is a central activity at the Writers' Group, and because of my re-visioning of it as a manifestation of "implicate order" (Bohm, 1980). I also introduce the neologism of "freewrighting" as a form of writing that constructs an artifact that can be later deconstructed or molded into other forms of writing.

I worked closely with four members from the group, each of whom had a personal interest in writing, longevity in the group, and a large body of writing collected over several years. I completed a series of in-depth interviews with each participant, collected and examined all their writings, and compiled participant-observer field notes. I then created narratives to evoke a sense of each writer's experience in the Writers' Group, interweaving a narrative way of knowing with a paradigmatic examination of the experience. I wanted to work with individuals from outside mainstream society because I believe that we have much to learn from exploring the edges, the margins, and the borders. It is often at these points of tension and contact that deep meaning is created. We have much to learn from writers who have been marginalized by society, through examining and discovering the value and meaning they ascribe to writing at the edge.

I explored the narratives, viewed from academic and theoretical contexts, to gain a deeper understanding of what it means for these writers to write from an expressive, personal perspective. I found that they created a sense of self through their writings, and their engagement in the act of writing allowed them an opportunity to explore personal perspectives on social issues. The act of writing, for these writers, was not simply to communicate ideas to others, the most common purpose for writing in academic institutions. Instead, they used writing to create a sense of who they were as people. In many ways, the writers constructed narratives of self through their writing. The writings, then, which were always read aloud to the group and discussed, became cultural artifacts that were examined as part of the complex social situation of the Writers' Group.

When you fall in the river
You are no longer a fisherman
You are a swimmer

I have been involved with the Canadian Mental Health Association Writers' Group for more than ten years. Each year we self-publish the collected writings of the participants and disseminate the books for everyone who attended the weekly sessions and submitted writing. Since we began the Writers' Group, over a hundred writers have attended at least one session, and the usual weekly attendance is between eight and fifteen writers. They range from teenagers to people in their late sixties, and usually an equal number of males and females attend each session. Membership in the group is extremely ethnically and racially varied, and though the majority are white, at least ten percent are Native American. Race, ethnicity, religious affiliation, and gender issues do not seem to be excluding factors in the Writers' Group. Instead, the Writers' Group seems to operate within an atmosphere that simply accepts difference. We have often addressed social, political, racial and gender issues in the writings and weekly discussions. This atmosphere of acceptance is essential to the group's success. As Bonnie [pseudonym] states, "Here, you are free to be who you are."

I have worked with several writing workshops over the last twenty years in Canada and the United States alongside professional and amateur writers, both as an active participant and as workshop leader or facilitator. I have also taught high school and university English and have utilized writing-process and writing-workshop techniques in my classes on many occasions. Although there are a great variety of ways to conduct writing workshops and writing groups, for the most part the experience entails some form of group response to individual pieces of writing. Usually a writer brings a piece of writing into the group environment after a draft is completed. The group members and teacher then critique the writing, and suggest improvement through group discussions and peer editing, as well as one-on-one editing sessions.

The practice of the Writers' Group generally follows what Graves (1973, 1975, 1983), Calkins (1986, 1991, 1994), and Atwell (1987, 1990) have espoused in their research and pedagogical practices. Writing is read and critiqued to make it stronger, more concise and more unified. There are some great advantages to approaching writing in this manner because the writer, presented with a reading audience that approximates what Fish (1980) calls an "interpretive community," is given immediate feedback about the writing. The feeling of community is very important for the members of the group, and several members have expressed that the group provides them with a sense of home.

The act of writing that occurs at the CMHA Writers' Group, however, is somewhat different from many writing-process and writing-workshop pedagogies and practices. Although a myriad of approaches to writing workshops exist, sessions usually focus on sharing and critiquing the writing that is brought to the writing workshop. In the CMHA Writers' Group, though a writer will occasionally bring in a piece of writing to read and receive comments, the usual pattern is for the writers to actually do the writing during the session. The writers focus on the act of writing, and then on the sharing of the resulting texts. In this way, the participants experience the act of writing very much as a social activity. After the writing, each writer voluntarily reads his or her work aloud to the other group members; it is not an issue if someone does not wish to share his or her work. Participants always have the right to pass, though they now rarely do. The act of writing and reading in the group seems to be of prime significance. The sharing of writing is extremely important to the writers, and the idea of community is central. The writing that results is, therefore, not only brought into the writing community and shared, it is actually, for the most part, created within the writing community.

The group meets in the board room of the Canadian Mental Health Association offices once each week for one-and-a-half to two hours. Like most of the activities at CMHA, we originally met from September through June, following the traditional school year; however, because of group insistence, we now meet twelve months a year. The room is actually quite simple in nature, and I'm not quite sure why it is called the board room, other than the board of the local branch of CMHA meets there once a month. The room could just as easily be called the activities room, or the large room, or the meeting room. Stacked against the wall are several folding tables, which we set up together in the middle of the room. In effect, this creates a circle in the square. We gather around the tables in order of arrival; there is no set seating arrangement.

One of my goals for the Writers' Group is to create a sense of responsibility within the group. Consequently the group is responsible for making coffee, organizing the tables, setting up the tables, putting the tables and chairs back where they were before we arrived, and making sure that all dishes are washed and put away. These small acts create a sense of ownership for the members of the Writers' Group.

We usually open the writing session with some conversation, and often simply talk about how our weeks went since the last time we met. Many of the members have little social interaction with anyone, and the talking helps connect, or re-connect, them with the rest of the group. We also might talk about a current news event, or a social or political issue that interests group members.

The sessions do not follow a prescribed formula, but in general we write on two or three topics each week. Topics are not imposed on the participants, though I constantly make suggestions, and keep a master list of topics that members have suggested in the past. The writers always have the option to write about anything that interests them. Sometimes I will start off a session with a writing heuristic, or word game, though usually I will suggest a topic and let them develop it as they wish. A simple suggestion such as "blue" can result in a poem, an autobiographical narrative, an essay, or lifewriting about past memories or dreams. I will occasionally give the writers a format to follow—a poetic structure, or a situation involving conflict, or a series of words that have to be used in the writing. The writers, of course, always have the option of doing what interests them, though usually they at least try writing using the suggestion, seeing it as a challenge, or a chance to play with language.

The individual writing sessions usually range in length from ten to twenty minutes, though I've also tried sessions as short as one minute, and as long as thirty. The time periods are quite flexible. The range of topics is extremely varied, and over the years we have written on hundreds of topics.

Sometimes in the middle of a writing session, I will stop, and just observe. But the experience goes far beyond the visual. There is an energy and concentration that is almost palpable. When the Writers' Group is writing, the room is completely quiet, except for the breathing of the writers and the scraping of pens against paper. Breath and paper. Each week it amazes me. It is often almost a spiritual experience. The act of writing, at this point, is similar to what Macrorie (1974, 1988) and Elbow (1973/1998, 1981) call freewriting. Individuals rarely suffer from "writer's block" and writing usually appears effortless.

After the writing is complete, we read and discuss what was written. We take turns, going around in a circle, with each writer reading what he or she has written. Writers always have the option of not reading, and this seems to ensure that they have the freedom to address any topic and not have to worry about social constrictions. Usually all the writers want to read; the sharing of their writing and giving voice to their words seem very important. Occasionally they will discuss their writing, focusing on both content and style. The suggestions are always made in an arena of mutual respect.

Some writing groups encourage a discussion before writing takes place to stimulate ideas on the topic, and to clarify the writer's thinking. This procedure is probably a carry-over from the adage, "clear thinking leads to clear writing." With the Writers' Group, the discussion usually occurs after the writing. This method can lead to some minor revisions or additions to the original writing; however, often what changes is not so much the specific piece of writing, but the perspective and mindset of the writer.

Elbow (1981) suggests that the writing process is actually two distinct and contradictory processes that often operate in opposition to each other: the creating process, and the critical process that is necessary for revising and editing. Much of the attention in the writing sessions of the Writers' Group is on the creative processes involved in the act of writing. This method differs from the pragmatic practices of many writing groups, which focus on critiquing the individual pieces of writing to improve them, with the group deciding the focus. I was once involved with a group of elderly writers who were very resistant to the idea of actually using "class time" to write. They felt that this was a complete waste of the time that should have been relegated to critiquing writing, and finding ideas on how to improve their writing. The Writers' Group members have a great desire to write and to share their writing with the rest of the group. The reading of writing is central to the success of the Writers' Group, and instead of focusing solely on the individual writer, the piece of writing, when read aloud, becomes part of the communal space. The writers in this group write to be read on an immediate level, as if they instinctively know that writing and reading, the writer and the reader, are intertwined in a communal act.

The Writers' Group

When we first started meeting, I found that I was sometimes interchanging the terms Writers' Group and Writing Group—a slight semantic shift. At first I thought the difference in meaning between Writing and Writers' was small, and probably insignificant, but the more I thought about it the more I realized that the semantic difference was of paramount importance to the writers.

What do I call the group that meets to write? The question becomes more than a semantic question; it becomes a central identity question. If the group is "The Writing Group," the focus of the group is on the activity of writing. "The Writing Group" is a group that writes—the "writing" in this case is a present participle acting as an adjective modifying the word "group." If the name of the group is the "Writers' Group," the focus is on the writers themselves, and not the activity of writing. The shift in semantic meaning may be slight to many people, but can profoundly shift the focus of attention.

To confirm this, I asked the group what they wanted to be called. There was absolutely no hesitation, and the response was unanimous: the group was to be called the Writers' Group.

"Why?" I asked.

"Because the Writers' Group is us."

"It belongs to us. We're very possessive of it."

"It isn't just an activity that we do."

"It is more than an activity."

"We are writers."

And that is what makes the group important. We are writers.

Chapter Two

Writing Theory and the Shift to Process

Writing-process theory, even if one focuses on the early theorists, is extremely diverse and complex; therefore, any historical summary of the process movement is bound to have serious omissions. It is important to remember that my goal in this chapter is to provide some of the theoretical underpinnings of how I engaged with the Writers' Group, and why I structured the writing sessions as I have. I have focused on personal writing, or what Britton (1970, 1975) called "writing in the expressive function," and have contextualized it within a larger theoretical structure of writing process. In the extant literature, much of the focus on the teaching and researching of writing is on its academic purpose, or what Bruner (1986, 1988, 1996) called "paradigmatic thinking." For this book, I used Bruner's concept of "narrative knowing" as a lens to examine writing-process theory. In exploring the value of writing for the members of the CMHA Writers' Group, I look at the aesthetic value of writing, and how the act of writing helps them develop a sense of who they are in relation to others, while negotiating meaning within social and cultural contexts. Narrative knowing is central to an understanding of the value of writing for these writers.

Over the past few decades there has been a subtle, yet profound shift in the way academics and teachers of writing view the nature of writing. In 1982, Maxine Hairston declared that a paradigm shift had occurred in the teaching of writing, as educators moved from a product-based approach to a writing-process approach. Hairston used Kuhn's (1962) historical examination of scientific revolution as a model to look at writing theory. Kuhn claimed that new evidence in science would eventually create a new paradigm that is "incommensurable" with what came before. Hairston adapted this model to claim that process theory has usurped the old model based on product. In hindsight, Hairston's claims can perhaps be viewed as hyperbole, though they are not without some validity, especially when one considers how process theory has affected classroom practice and pedagogy. Changes in contemporary composition theory have been incorporated into current curriculum design and classroom practices, with an emphasis on writing process and the writing workshop. Changes in the teaching of writing are ongoing, and there remains a need to understand further the nature of this paradigm shift, and what it means to use a process approach in the teaching of writing.

David Bohm has analyzed Kuhn's ideas to show how humans can create fragmentation in their thinking, perspective, and analysis by not incorporating older ideas into the new paradigms. Bohm suggests, "It is therefore important to question Kuhn's whole analysis of this incommensurability and ask if such a fundamental dislocation of ideas must always accompany a scientific revolution" (Bohm & Peat, 2000, p. 27). Perhaps changes in writing theory have created a similar fragmentation. In many ways, humans appear to think in binaries and this often results in oversimplification. It is much more difficult to exist in paradox and contradiction, but maybe that is where true meaning is constructed.

Hairston attempts to impose Kuhn's analysis of science paradigms on developments in composition or writing theory by using the metaphor of winds of change sweeping away the old and bringing on the new. It is this perspective that has led to much fragmentation in the field of writing theory and composition pedagogy. We get trapped in a series of binary loops: product versus process, process versus genres, personal versus academic, personal versus social. Perhaps much is to be learned by implementing both sides of the binary, and not ignoring either perspective. Much process pedagogy often ignores the significance of the content, and the meaning that content has for the individual writer. Much personal writing pedagogy ignores the influence of social issues and pressure. Much academic writing ignores the intersection of the individual writer's own interest with the content and genre. Much genre theory focuses on structure rather than the specific significance of that structure for a specific purpose for an individual writer. Theorists and educationists get caught in a "non-negotiable position," again to borrow from Bohm. We need to actively engage in a dialogue that incorporates different voices and perspectives. This book attempts to address issues of diversity by not ignoring contradictions.

Early Writing-Process Theory

Any narrative of a theoretical movement is obviously only one perspective of many possibilities. I do not pretend that the following is authoritative in any way. My intention is to provide a contextual background for my work in reconsidering the value of personal, or expressive, writing. My intent is to eventually demonstrate that the seemingly simple and isolated act of personal writing is actually a very complex social engagement.

Tobin, in the introduction to *Taking Stock: The Writing Process Movement in the 90's*, summarizes the writing process movement:

> Every single written product is the result of *some* process—and almost every process leads to some sort of product. But in the composition world, the term has come to mean something else: an *emphasis* on the process, student choice and voice, revision, self-expression. But most of all it has come to mean a critique (or even outright rejection) of traditional, product-driven, rules-based, correctness-obsessed writing instruction. The process movement, then, has been a rejection of a particular kind of product—the superficial, formulaic essays that most of us grew up writing and teaching—and a particular kind of process—write, proofread, hand in, and then move on to next week's assignment. (Tobin & Newkirk, 1994, p. 5)

The writing process movement started to shift the focus from an emphasis on essay structures, text, grammar and themes to the interests of the individual writer and how he or she created, valued and processed writing. The movement to understand the needs of individual writers is central to this shift in thinking. Of course, it is important to remember that any "paradigm shift" is really a series of incremental changes. The early work of Holbrook (1964, 1967, 1979), Murray (1968), and Macrorie (1970, 1974) began considering students as individuals in a larger social situation, and not simply as faceless components of a class, grade, school, society, or culture.

Educators began looking at how individual writers processed ideas into a final product. Britton (1972) saw the writing process as a three-step model: conception, incubation, and production. This structural model corresponds to that of Rohman (1965), another early process theorist, and his three-stage writing model: pre-write, write, and re-write. This theoretical shift led to changes in pedagogic practice. For instance, if writing occurred in stages, then teaching the stages of writing in the classroom had distinct advantages over a product-oriented approach.

Emig (1971), in her study of the writing habits of grade-twelve students, was one of the first researchers to examine the writing process. Using her background in literature, she used anecdotal stories of how professional writers created final texts to relate how grade-twelve students were able to conceptualize writing. She found that the twelfth-graders in her sample engaged "in two modes of composing—reflexive and extensive—characterized by processes of different lengths with different clustering of components" (p. 91). One of her findings was that the writers did not always follow a linear sequence when writing, and that especially during "self-sponsored" or "reflexive" writing, the process was more often hesitant, recursive, and difficult to trace (pp. 92-93). Emig also noted that "extensive writing occurs chiefly as prose; the attitude toward the field of discourse is often detached and reportorial. Adult others, notably teachers, are the chief audience for extensive writing" (p. 91). This observation is very similar to Britton et al.'s (1975) findings that about ninety-five percent of all sampled writing was written with the teacher as its intended audience (p. 131). Reflexive writing, on the other hand, was usually directed at the self as the chief audience, though occasionally the writing was given to a trusted peer.

The acceptance of Emig's study led to a major shift in focus away from the study of writing as product toward the writing process itself. Researchers started conceptualizing how the writing process worked in practice. Donald Graves (1973, 1975, 1983, 1994), Nancie Atwell (1987, 1990), and Lucy Calkins (1983, 1986, 1991) were among the first to bring the movement to elementary and middle-years schools. At the university level, Donald Murray (1968, 1984, 1985), James Moffett (1968, 1973), Peter Elbow (1973/1998, 1981, 2000), and Ken Macrorie (1970, 1974, 1980, 1988) began using process theory in their teaching. Murray developed one-to-one conferencing, writing to learn, and lived by the slogan "Teach writing as a process, not a product!" (Quoted in Tobin & Newkirk, 1994, p. 3). Murray added, "Writing is above all a process. It is a logical sequence of activities that can be understood by anyone" (1984, p. 6). Ken Macrorie (1974) and Peter Elbow (1973/1998) developed the use of freewriting as means of opening up student writing to the writer within. I will develop this idea in a later chapter because of its prevalence within the writing activities of the Writers' Group.

The Dartmouth Conference in 1966, where British educators such as Britton connected and communicated with American educators, was a seminal event in the process writing movement. American and British composition instructors started looking more seriously at their students' writing and how it was created. Writing teachers began including process theory in their teaching, often based on the underpinnings of expressivist or reflexive writing, and sometimes without completely understanding writing-process theory.

With writing theory moving from product to process, the pedagogy of teaching writing began to change as well, moving from product writing assignments to the validation of the writing process and the idea of the writers' workshop. Practical implementations were the work of such practitioners as Moffett (1973), Murray (1968, 1984, 1985), Graves (1973, 1975, 1983), Calkins (1983, 1986) and Atwell (1987, 1990).

Writing-process theory and writing workshop concepts have become popular pedagogical practices in curriculum guides, textbooks and academic journals in English language arts. Many of the latest North American curriculum guides use writing-process theory and writing workshops as basic assumptions and underlying frameworks. Writing-process theory is extremely valuable in terms of planning and organizing, and seeing writing as a means of discovery; however, the theory remains in need of further examination. For instance, writing-process pedagogical practice has sometimes led to a partial rejection of the importance of the final product, as well as sometimes ignoring the value of the writing content and final product to the individual writers. As well, the common writing process practiced by many writing teachers is still focused on revisions of the product, or the future product, instead of the writing process of the individual writer. The five-step model of the writing process has been almost standardized in many cases, both by textbook writers and teachers. A typical example of this can be found in Tompkins' (2000) widely used university textbook for teachers of writing, *Teaching Writing: Balancing Process and Product*. Though the book attempts to balance process with the final product, the assumption is that writing is a process based on a number of limited steps. Teachers usually interpret these steps to be sequential, and in extreme cases, use the five steps of the writing process to correspond to the five days of the school week.

There has been little work done on the actual creative process involved in writing, or how the process progresses and develops. Flower and Hayes (1981) claim that the writing process as a stage model offers

> an inadequate account of the more intimate, moment-by-moment intellectual process of composing. How, for example, is the output of one stage, such as pre-writing or incubation, transferred to the next?...Such models are typically silent on the inner processes of decision and choice. (p. 367)

Flower and Hayes, like many other cognitivist theorists, have searched for a linear, sequential model of how writers conceive and create writing. With my study I move beyond a strictly paradigmatic analysis of writing, and include a narrative perspective of writing as an alternative way of knowing.

With the study of the Writers' Group I explored the inner processes that Flower and Hayes mentioned, but from a very different perspective. In later sections I show how Csikszentmihalyi's (1990, 1993, 1997) work with flow and creative processing has great relevance to the reconceptualization of freewriting and expressive writing. Csikszentmihalyi defines flow as the "state in which people are so involved in an activity that nothing else seems to matter; the experience is so enjoyable that people will do it even at great cost, for the sheer sake of doing it" (1990, p. 4). At the Writers' Group, the act of writing becomes an act of pure joy, and though each writer seemingly works alone, the process is actually quite social. Writing is both an individual and a social act. Writing theory is in constant need of re-thinking, re-conceptualizing, and re-theorizing. Tobin notes that

> contemporary composition critics are right when they point out that early writing process advocates did not pay much attention to the larger cultural and social influences on individual writers; that the movement has, for the most part, posited "the writer" in a way that erases difference of race, class, gender, personality; and, finally, that in some cases writing process pedagogy has simply replaced one mechanistic process with another: "First you brainstorm, then freewrite, then draft, revise, edit." (Tobin & Newkirk, 1994, p. 8)

Here is a good summation of a series of the limitations of early writing-process theory. A writer, even when working alone, is always influenced by outside forces. To consider a writer as an isolated individual who utilizes a cognitive process to write is somewhat naïve. Bizzell in her article "Cognition, convention, and certainty: What we need to know about writing," originally published in 1982, suggested that educators need to consider both individual and social factors. Bizzell (1992) suggests, "answers to what we need to know about writing will have to come from both the inner-directed and the outer-directed theoretical schools if we wish to have a complete picture of the composing process" (p. 81). Faigley (1986, 1992) and Berlin (1987, 1988, 1990) both critique early writing-process theory, especially that which they label expressivist, as being somewhat simplistic in its Romantic vision of the self as an autonomous being. In my work with the Writers' Group we don't ignore cultural and social influences. Instead we actively engage issues of race, class, gender, power and personality. In doing so, we create personal writing in a zone of diversity and acceptance, within a culture of difference.

My research project, working with writers from outside the typical school system and curriculum, has allowed me to explore more freely the value of personal writing, and how it relates to the writing process. Writing is never a simple, isolated event; instead, it is a highly complex social act. Rosenblatt (1988) recognized the need to acknowledge the social complexity of the writer's environment, and the social dimensions of the writing act itself. Rosenblatt considered the complexity of working with texts within a social environment:

> Writing, we know, is always an event in time, occurring at a particular moment in the writer's biography, in particular circumstances, under particular pressures, external as well as internal. In short, the writer is always transacting with a personal, social, and cultural environment. (We shall see that the writer transacts also with the very text being produced.) Thus the writing process must be seen as always embodying both personal and social, or individual and environmental, factors. (1988, p. 7)

Even something as seemingly simple as freewriting, as espoused by such writing teachers as Macrorie (1970, 1974, 1988) and Elbow (1973/1998), can be construed as a much more complex cognitive process. Rosenblatt suggests that freewriting "should be seen as a technique for tapping the linguistic reservoir unhampered by anxieties about acceptability of subject, sequence, or mechanics" (1988, p. 7). Seen in this way, freewriting permits "elements of the experiential stream, verbal components of memory, and present concerns, to rise to consciousness" (Rosenblatt, 1988, p. 7). A writer, even when seemingly acting alone, is always part of a larger social environment. The creation of a text does not occur in a social vacuum. Writing is a social act that always occurs within a specific discourse community (Bakhtin, 1986). As well, Vygotsky (1930/1978) has noted that the process of putting experience into language is a meaning-making process, which always functions within a social context.

In the realm of writing-workshop practice, Lensmire (1994a, 1994b, 1998, 2000) is often critical of writing group advocates and writing process as it is currently taught in many school systems. Using a critical theorist's perspective, he has critiqued the limitations of writing-workshop and writing-process pedagogy. Lensmire believes that many writing teachers ignore the complexities of modern society and such forces as sexism, racism and classism. Many writing groups use an inaccurate and potentially dangerous vision of the child as Romantic visionary. Each writer, in this perspective, is nurtured through the writing in a cooperative process that is eventually shared in a public forum of mutual admiration. Lensmire is not alone in believing that this perspective is naïve and simplistic. Willinsky (1990) is also highly critical of the Romantic vision in his book, *The New Literacy: Redefining Reading and Writing in the Schools*.

Lensmire introduces the darker side of the writing workshop, and the writing process. Teachers sometimes misrepresent what it means to write and what it means to live in a multi-perspective, postmodern world by ignoring complex social realities. Teachers cannot ignore the inequalities that are prevalent in our society. Sexism, racism, and economic classism all exist, and it is both naïve and damaging to ignore these factors.

Fine (1987) and Delpit (1988, 1995) show that the dominant hegemony subtly, but very effectively, silences the disenfranchised. The dominant culture coerces minorities to adapt the dominant values, with the schools as a controlling force. Within the context of the writing workshop, subtle forces encourage writers to conform. There is a similar force at work in university writing programs: radical or non-conforming work is often leveled out through revision and class discussion. Any offensive or distinctive aspects, which often make a piece of writing unique, are edited out, resulting in a final product that is dull and lifeless. In the school system, writing is shaped to reflect a respectable voice, even if that voice is false or limiting. Lensmire, in his work with elementary school students, exposes some of the dangers of the writing workshop, especially regarding the validation of voice. Many students are unable to explore ideas because of a teacher's perception of the inappropriateness of the writing within the social situation.

It is obvious that issues of power, race, gender, and acceptable discourse communities influence writing, and perhaps the writers themselves. In this book, I propose that personal writing is also a site of significant negotiation, and always operates in what I call the riparian zone. Accordingly, I want to reconsider what it means to write in the expressive function.

James Britton's Writing Functions

The writing theories of James Britton (1970, 1972, 1979, 1980), especially his concept of the three writing functions: transactional, poetic and expressive, have been vastly underestimated in the last few years, and yet many composition researchers have, consciously or unconsciously, adapted and extended his ideas in their work, thus providing a framework for many contemporary theoretical constructs in the study of writing. The longitudinal study by scholars from the London School of Education, *The Development of Writing Abilities (11–18)*, (Britton, Burgess, Martin, McLeod & Rosen, 1975), examined the different functions of language used, as well as the intended audiences addressed, by British students in their writing assignments.

A simplified explanation of Britton's construct would show a continuum of language use with transactional language at one extreme, expressive language in the middle, and poetic or aesthetic language at the other extreme. Transactional writing informs, persuades, and instructs, and is always concerned with an end outside of itself. Expressive writing uses language that is "close to the self" (Britton, 1972, p. 96) and verbalizes the writer's consciousness. Poetic writing is "a verbal construct, an 'object' made out of language. The words themselves, and all they refer to, are selected to make an arrangement, a formal pattern" (Britton et al., 1975, p. 90). Britton believed that all writing starts from the expressive and can develop from that point:

> Development comes in two main directions—towards the transactional and towards the poetic. And in either case, if we are successful, children will continue to write *as themselves* as they reach those two poles. Their explorations of the outer world demand the transactional; their explorations of the inner world demand the poetic, and the roots of it all remain in the expressive. (Britton, 1972, p. 110)

Although Britton's ideas probably originated from a humanist or Romantic view of language expressing an inner self, I maintain that Britton's concept of expressive writing still holds from a postmodern, or poststructuralist perspective. Expressive language may relate to a "fixed" self, a "developing" self, or even a multiplicity of selves.

A central idea in Britton's work is the difference between the writer as participant and the writer as spectator. Britton built much of his thinking in this area on the earlier work of D. W. Harding (1937), the British psychologist, who introduced the idea of spectator and participant in reading theory. In Britton's constructed model of the functions of writing, transactional language operates with the writer in the participant role, while poetic language operates with the writer as spectator. In Britton's taxonomy, the spectator role has far more possibilities. Britton (1970) published some of his thinking on this role in the booklet *Explorations in Children's Writing*:

> If one accepts the general thesis that man does not respond directly to experiences, but builds from his experience a representation of the world, then it follows that two courses are open to him. He can respond to the real world, operate in the real world, via the representation; or he can operate directly upon the representation itself. That is, in fact, my basic distinction between being a participant and a spectator. And what I have stressed has been the importance of the spectator role activity, both in reading literature and in writing it. (p. 63)

Britton concluded by suggesting that as "participants we only have one life; as spectators, an infinite number is open to us" (p. 58). As writers, we have infinite possibilities to explore the world through engagements with text as both representation and evocation.

Britton's theoretical framework provided a very useful foundation to examine the writing that occurs in the CMHA Writers' Group. The group members seem to begin most of their writing from the expressive function, but with greater confidence and self-awareness, the function changes over time, moving to what Britton describes as transactional and poetic writing. Expressive language was central in Britton's study, and in his resulting thinking on writing. Britton believed that the "kinds of writing first used effectively by the young writer appear to be essentially personal; the last kinds to be acquired (if they ever are) are those scientific and social uses of language which appear to be essentially impersonal" (Britton et al., 1975, p. 5). Britton claimed that expressive writing was an under-utilized form of writing and that "learning could be improved if fuller use were made of the heuristic potential of expressive writing" (1979, p. 129).

Britton suggested that we "talk and we write about experience...in order to shape it and incorporate it into the body of our past experiences" (1970, p. 56). Britton's ideas are quite profound:

> What is organized is far more than words. What is organized is the fabric of experience as we represent it to ourselves in sight and sound, in emotional colour, and so on. What is organized is far more than words, but words provide the means by which we organize it. It often happens that as we try to recall an event, to revive some vague memory, we find ourselves searching for a word, the name of a place or a person perhaps. And with the word, when we have found it, the whole thing comes into focus. It is as though language were the Ariadne's thread by which we penetrate the maze. (p. 56)

It is as if through the use of language, especially writing, experience is clarified and finally understood, and the self conceptualized.

Moffett (1968, 1973) covered similar territory with his research work in the United States on the value of writing and student-centered education. Though he is often considered to follow a cognitive-developmental approach to writing, the heart of his pedagogy is the importance of self in the writing:

> I recommend training the student to write for the class group, which is the nearest to a contemporary world-at-large; accustoming him to having his themes read and discussed workshop fashion; and asking him to write about raw material from his own experience which he is motivated to write about and to invent an appropriate rhetoric for. It is amazing how much so-called writing problems clear up when the student really cares, when he is realistically put into the drama of somebody with something to say to somebody else. (Moffett, 1968, p. 12)

Moffett suggested that educators always contextualize the writing assignments, taking into account the student as an "I" writing about a meaningful "what" for a specific reason and for a relevant audience (Moffett, 1968, p. 12). Moffett's idea of using raw material from the writer's own experience is very similar to Britton's (1970, 1975) idea of expressive writing. Rather than focusing writing assignments on irrelevant and abstract topics, Moffett believed that the use of personal ideas often leads to meaningful writing.

In their longitudinal study, Britton et al. (1975) found that transactional (informational) writing was by far the most dominant category used in schools, accounting for roughly two-thirds of the writing in the sample (p. 163). Of the other two writing functions in Britton's taxonomy, the researchers found that:

> the proportion occupied by expressive writing (5.5%) is low to the point of marginality, while that occupied by poetic writing, though more significant, is no more than 17.6%. As a rough and ready way of describing this overall configuration we can say that there is three times as much transactional writing as both of the other functions put together,

and approximately thirteen times as much transactional writing as expressive. (Britton et al., 1975, p. 163)

Expressive writing, as Britton conceived it, continues to be an underdeveloped mode of writing in most academic settings. Some recent studies have suggested that the development of expressivist or personal writing that is "close to the self" leads to greater skills and abilities in other language functions. Allen (2000) maintains that after students master effective personal essays (expressive function), their academic writing (transactional function) also improves because the personal essay "confronts writers with responsibility for making meaning. Form follows substance" (p. 281).

Britton maintained that expressive language is "a kind of matrix from which differentiated forms of mature writing are developed" (Britton et al., 1975, p. 83). It is at this point, where the writer is meaningfully engaged, that educators could introduce other writing genres and structures. In this sense, Britton was perhaps correct when he suggested that writing in the expressive function was the matrix for the other functions; however, there is a need to demonstrate or show the other more structured writing functions to students. The shift to other writing functions is not a "natural" progression as some educators have assumed, and exposure to other discourses, and other language structures is necessary.

Freewriting and Writing Theory

One of the dominant writing activities employed at the Writers' Group is freewriting. It appears that freewriting is an activity that lends itself best to writing in the expressive function. In this chapter, I look at freewriting as part of writing theory, and provide a brief historical context. Later in the book, I reexamine freewriting in light of the experiences of the writers from the CMHA Writers' Group, and begin to reconceptualize its significance as a writing activity.

Freewriting, at least in terms of composition theory, can probably be traced to Ken Macrorie (1974). In *A Vulnerable Teacher* he relates the beginnings of the idea:

> For seventeen years I heard my students repeating badly to me what I had said to them and hundreds before them. I read their tired, hurriedly written papers conveying in academic dialect what they thought proper to give Teacher. One day in May in an Advanced Writing class I finally exploded. "I can't stand to read this junk any longer. Go back and write down as fast as you can whatever is in your mind for fifteen minutes. Write so fast you can't think of punctuation or spelling or how you're going to say it. I would like for a change to read some truth that counts for you."

> Since that day in 1964 I have turned my teaching around. Now in every course I begin by asking students to write anything that comes to their mind. Freed of limitations and prohibitions common to academic writing assignments, they find unsuspected powers....I was no longer hearing my words and thoughts coming back to me. (Macrorie, 1974, pp. 5-6)

Macrorie utilized freewriting as part of his pedagogy for most of his career as a way of helping his English students reach a deeper level of writing that went beyond the superficial. Macrorie (1980) writes:

> If you're free-writing well, you'll concentrate so hard on truthtelling and write so fast you'll put yourself into a kind of trance, like that between waking and sleeping at night (or sleeping and waking in the morning) when a gaggle of good ideas or memories comes together for you....You'll be writing sentences that make sense and they'll flow into each other with the logic of mind or feeling. (p. 7)

Peter Elbow (1973/1998), who is usually considered one of the first practitioners of freewriting because of the influence of *Writing Without Teachers*, gives credit and thanks to Ken Macrorie in the introduction of the second edition:

> I thanked him in the introduction [of the 1973 edition], but let me say a little more. I first learned about freewriting from him....I feel the whole profession is indebted to his blunt, feisty bravery—his constant fight against baloney....He took a lot of criticism because he never trimmed his sails to prevailing fashion. His tough stance made it easier for others of us afterwards to be braver than we could have been—and at smaller personal and professional cost. (Elbow, 1973/1998, p. xxviii)

Of course, most innovations happen in context. Freewriting, in many ways, could be construed as an educational application of automatic writing as was many writers practiced at the turn of the century, including those in the Dadaist and Surrealist movements. Brotchie (1995), in *Surrealist Games*, describes automatic writing:

> Sit at a table with pen and paper; put yourself in a "receptive" frame of mind, and start writing. Continue writing without thinking of what is appearing beneath your pen. Write as fast as you can. If, for some reason, the flow stops, leave a space and immediately begin again by writing down the first letter of the next sentence. Choose this letter at random before you begin, for instance, a "t", and always begin this new sentence with a "t". Although in the purest version of automatism nothing is "corrected" or rewritten, the unexpected material produced by this method can be used as the basis for further composition. What is crucial is the unpremeditated free association that creates the basic text. (via http://www.duke.edu/web/lit132/automatic.html)

Freewriting could also be considered an extension of James Joyce's concept of stream of consciousness as used in his novels. The Beat writers also utilized automatic writing, or uncensored writing, to reach and reveal deeper levels of thinking they felt were often constrained by social convention. Jack Kerouac, in his "Essentials of Spontaneous Prose," explains the procedure:

> Time being of the essence in the purity of speech, sketching language is undisturbed flow from the mind of personal secret idea-words, blowing (as per jazz musician) on subject of image. (cited in Charters, 1992, p. 57)

Kerouac wanted to approximate the flow of music in his writing, especially the improvisational nature of jazz. Many Beat writers wanted to push conventional methods of composing. Early in his career, poet Kenneth Rexroth suggested that Allen Ginsberg should write to please himself. Ginsberg, who decided to experiment with Kerouac's ideas of spontaneous prose, recalls:

> I thought I wouldn't write a poem but just write what I wanted to without fear, let my imagination go, open secrecy, and scribble magic lines from my real mind—sum up my life—something I wouldn't be able to show anybody, writ for my own soul's ear and a few other golden ears. (Ginsberg cited in Charters, 1992, p. 61)

Allen Ginsberg's maxim "first thought, best thought" reflects a Buddhist mindset that differs from a strict linear, sequential format of conception. Ginsberg understood writing as an extension of his mind at a specific moment in his life (personal communication, November 15, 1988).

It is possible that we have underestimated the value of the act of writing itself. We have imposed a rational, sequential, hierarchical concept to writing, beginning with the assumption that thinking leads to writing, and then one step leads logically the next, to a process that often occurs in almost Zen-like moments of holistic understanding.

It is perhaps time to reconsider the significance of freewriting in writing pedagogy. Freewriting, in most accounts of writing-process theory, is seen as a pre-writing activity or heuristic, done before a writer actually writes as a practice run, or a place to get started, or as an activity to "get the juices flowing." The following quotation is representative of many writing texts:

> Children use a variety of writing activities to gather and organize ideas before beginning to draft their compositions. They brainstorm words and images, sequence lists of events, cluster main ideas and details, make other charts or diagrams to record ideas, or quickwrite to discover what they know about a topic and what direction their writing might take. Outlining is another form of prewriting, but this traditional prewriting activity is less effective than clustering and not recommended for younger students. (Tompkins, 2000, p. 15)

In much writing-process theory, quickwriting, or freewriting, is considered a prewriting activity, or preliminary discovery and exploring activity, and is not considered an act of writing in itself that results in a final product. Freewriting is usually perceived as a means of helping students "get into" writing, or "find their true voice," or to improve their writing through practice. The following extract from Romano's (1987) *Clearing the Way* neatly summarizes much current thinking about the value of freewriting:

> In any writing class, then, the first and constant order of business is to enable all students to establish and develop their individual voices. Teachers must cut them loose the first day. Let them write in any form they choose. But make sure they write and sustain that writing long enough to rev up their voices. Ken Macrorie (1976) and Peter Elbow call such activity "freewriting." Donald Murray (1983) has called it "following a line of language."
>
> Call it whatever you like. Just be sure to cut students loose. Let them write rapidly and frequently for a set amount of time...without regard to error, expectation, or self. Let them and you find out what they sound like when they know their words will not be marked wrong, when adhering to a particular form is not the prime requirement, when failure is an impossibility.
>
> Such free or nonstop writing should be a staple in every English class. Its objective, its goal, is the development of fluency and self-confidence—the parents of voice. Plenty of honest language production—fluency—is the sole criterion for successful freewriting. Quality of language production is not. But even so, frequent engagement in rapid writing will improve the quality of writing. (pp. 7-8)

Macrorie (1976) claims that:

> Free writing is practice. It involves no pressure on the practicer. It never requires perfection. If the practicer goofs, he has not lost the game or produced a work disgraceful in the public eye. He can forget the bad shots. They do not penalize him. If a writer produces a good passage, he can show it to other persons because he has it down on paper. He is luckier than the golfer, who cannot take a shot off the practice tee home to show the family. (p. 11-12)

Elbow (1973/1998) also sees freewriting as a means of practicing writing:

> The most effective way I know to improve your writing is to do freewriting exercises regularly. At least three times a week. They are sometimes called "automatic writing," "babbling" or "jabbering" exercises. The idea is simply to write for ten minutes (later on, perhaps fifteen or twenty). Don't stop for anything. Go quickly without rushing. Never stop to look back, to cross something out, to wonder how to spell something, to wonder what word or thought to use, or to think about what you are doing. If you can't think of a word or a spelling, just use a squiggle or else write, "I can't think of it." Just put down something. The easiest thing is just to put down whatever is in your mind. If you

get stuck it's fine to write, "I can't think what to say, I can't think what to say" as many times as you want; or repeat the last word you wrote over and over again; or anything else. The only requirement is that you never stop. (p. 3)

Elbow further suggests that "writing badly, then, is a crucial part of learning to write well. Indeed, regressing and falling apart are a crucial and usually necessary part of any complex leaning" (p. 136).

Donald Murray (1999), another prominent early writing process theorist, is also a believer in freewriting:

> I began, as usual, by babbling. Some call this *free writing*: putting words on paper without editing or even stopping to correct spelling or grammar. I prefer *Washington Post* feature writer Cynthia Gorney's description: "I start to babble, sometimes starting in the middle of the story and usually fairly quickly I see how it's going to start. It just starts shaping itself. I tell students, 'Don't think, write.'" (p. 300)

Freewriting is rarely seen as means of creating a product in itself, and I think that needs to be examined. Instead of looking at freewriting as practice, or sloppy or non-thoughtful writing, we could instead see freewriting as a different strand of writing. When a piece of writing is finished, even if it is thought of as a draft, or a practice run, it becomes a product, or artifact. As soon as the writing becomes an artifact, it can be manipulated, or re-formed, or reconceptualized. The writing can also be enjoyed, savored and honored.

Perhaps freewriting has a deeper pedagogical significance. Peter Elbow has recently started to reexamine his thinking about freewriting. In the essay "Toward a phenomenology of freewriting," Elbow (2000) confirms the value of freewriting in his teaching pedagogy:

> I must admit to myself and to others that freewriting may be what I care about most in writing and teaching writing. I learn most from it. I get my best ideas and writing from it. I get my best group and community work done that way. I feel most myself when I freewrite. I think freewriting helps my students more than anything else I show them, and they usually agree with me over the years in formal and informal evaluations....I'm bemused that I work so hard teaching complicated ideas and procedures, yet at the end they say they learned most from what I taught them in the first half hour of the first class (though I use it extensively throughout the term). (pp. 113–114)

But why is freewriting so important and successful in his teaching practice? Elbow then does some rumination about how and why freewriting seems to work so well in his writing classes, and begins to look at the social aspects of the activity:

> Freewriting is always private—by definition, for the sake of safety. But I have come to feel an intriguing link between freewriting and sociability because I so often do this private

> writing in the company of others—with a class or a workshop. Thus true freewriting "by the book," never pausing, has come in certain ways to feel like a companionable activity: one sits there writing for oneself but hears other people's pens and pencils moving across the paper, people moving in their chairs, sometimes a grunt or sigh or giggle. The effect of using these conditions for freewriting (however private) is to contradict the association of writing with isolation. (p. 120)

I have witnessed similar responses at the Writers' Group when they are completely involved in the act of writing. The Writers' Group is very much a social group. But as I have suggested earlier, it is not simply that the members enjoy the social aspects of writing as a group; it is also the adventure of the writing itself that draws them. Elbow (2000) starts to look at what is involved in the process of freewriting:

> There is another experience that is central to my involvement with freewriting and that is the sense of *letting go*...When I freewrite I let go, stop steering, drop the balls and allow things to come to me—just babble onto paper. It's the difference between Linda Flower's emphasis on always making a plan and trying to follow it versus plunging along with no plan; between trying to steer versus letting go of the steering wheel and just letting words come. (p. 130)

The idea of "letting go," or surrender, is central to freewriting especially, as Elbow (2000) notes, "when one manages to invite the momentum of language or one's larger mind or whatever to take over. Freewriting is an invitation to stop writing and instead to 'be written'" (p. 131). This idea could have deep philosophical ramifications if what is being written is the "self."

Expressive Writing and the Social Discourse of Writing Groups

At the Writers' Group, we use freewriting as a central activity. Most of the resulting writing could be categorized as expressive writing, which Britton believed was writing that was close to the "self." Yet Britton seems to assume that a "self" is a clearly defined entity that simply needs to be recognized or discovered—he doesn't appear to explore the relationship of an individual to others, and how expressive writing relates to cultural and social forces. In this book, I explore the significance of expressive writing within the social situation of a writing group, and how the individual writers make meaning within that social context.

Originally, writing groups were considered socially neutral because they were designed to promote individual writers and their writing abilities. Recently scholars have given more consideration to the social aspects of writing groups—as discourse communities, and the sites of social and political influence.

Though there is no direct connection between writing-process theory and the advent of writing groups, the two concepts appear to have developed in tandem as process theory was pedagogically implemented. As individual writers were validated, the teacher was no longer the lone hierarchical authority figure. Peer editing and peer conferencing became central—partially as a means of validating the students' authority, but also as a practical means of classroom management because the teacher authority couldn't be everywhere at once. In many ways, Vygotsky's (1930/1978) concept of "the zone of proximal development" became a part of daily praxis in small group and cooperative learning.

Writing Groups moved from the classroom into various adult programs for several reasons including literacy issues, as well as social and political empowerment. Adult writing groups at seniors' homes, prisons, and night classes in many ways created subtle political and social forces of empowerment, and often a sense of community. The CMHA Writers' Group is a unique and valuable research site for exploring writing theory because it provides an opportunity to witness how individual writers utilize personal writing in a complex social situation. The writing created at the Writers' Group is completely dependent on the interest and motivation of the writers involved. Because the Writers' Group operates completely outside the usual parameters of institutional learning or business, the writing that occurs is different from that produced for academic, or business, or communication purposes. Research on writing and writing workshops that operates beyond the scope of academic or business institutions is surprisingly rare.

Dreher (1980) worked with a relatively healthy population of elderly writers in a retirement village using a highly structured format, based on a four-part sequence of activities: lecture, participation, reading aloud, and writing assignments. She based much of her rationale for teaching elderly writers on the work of Robert H. Butler, M.D., chairman of the National Council of Aging. Butler claimed that reviewing and writing about the past, which he called life review, helped "resolve conflicts and regrets and reconcile personal relationships...because writers gain insight into their purposes for living and integrate them into the present and future" (quoted in Dreher, 1980, p. 54). Dreher mentioned that as the class progressed "the group requested 'homework,' not just because it was conventional, but because they wanted to practice, to share their work with teachers and peers, and to be commended" (p. 55). Dreher also notes that although only one person undertook a long-term project, the "number of pages handed in [by the group] increased, so lectures became considerably shorter and participation much longer" (p. 56). The initial assignments led to a drive to write more to gain an understanding of the participants' own lives.

Koch (1977) taught poetry to elderly people in a nursing home in New York City with surprisingly good results. His writers, all in their seventies, eighties, and nineties and from working-class backgrounds with limited education, were all "incapacitated in some way, by illness or old age" (p. 3). Yet by the end of the workshop all were actively writing poetry with enthusiastic involvement and participation. Koch states:

> The strength and beauty of what they had to say, once they had said it, made it clear what had been neglected....These things were in our students, but, I suspect, for the most part hidden. Writing poems, they discovered them and made them into art. They were richer for that, and so, to a different degree, were those who heard their poems and read them. (p. 57)

The writing and the interaction within the group led to a sense of richness and value in the writers' own lives.

Staples (1981) taught a writing course "to persons over 55 under the auspices of the Institute of Lifetime Learning, a nonprofit, self-supporting institution associated with Austin Community College" (p. 1). She found that the writing course for elders had a potential to "open new horizons for teachers [and] valuably extend a continuing education curriculum" (p. 13), as well as provide to the writers "the learning, discovery, and self awareness that study in the humanities can uniquely provide" (p. 13). She found that the elderly writers were "willing to participate actively" and were "motivated by interests, by inner rewards" (p. 12) and that the writers' intellectual interests were personal, not academic (p. 6). Staples found that the "motivation in such a group does not depend on externals—like credit, grades, or even teacher approval—but on friendship, shared ideas, and new writing experiences" (pp. 6-7). Because of the personal nature of the writing and the writers' motivation for involvement in the course, Staples believed that her job as writing instructor was to "acknowledge each member according to his or her needs" (p. 7).

Gillis and Wagner (1980) were involved in a 1977-78 model project of the Workshops for the Aged, funded by grants from the Michigan Councils for the Humanities and Arts. Michigan State University's Department of English administered the project, *Life-Writing for Life-Living, Autobiography for Senior Citizens*. One goal of the writing project was to address the marginalization of elderly people in modern society, and through writing provide them with the means to a better sense of self-worth and social involvement. Gillis and Wagner state:

> Old people are a neglected minority in the United States. They are given few opportunities to participate in or contribute directly to the enrichment of our culture. Alienation from society at large and a cultural devaluing of aging are factors contributing to a

decreased sense of self-worth in elderly people. This decreased self-worth may in itself be enormously debilitating, and, coupled with physical handicaps associated with aging, may interfere with old people's abilities to lead creative and mentally healthy lives. (p. 4)

The project conducted writing workshops in seniors' residential and day-care centers in which the activities were designed "to stimulate reminiscence and sharing of personal history and experiences, culminating in oral and/or written compositions—narrative, stories, poetry" (p. 4). They believed that "recognizing the value of one's past is requisite to the confidence that precedes creativity and learning" (p. 4). The project provided elderly residents an environment in which they could "reminisce, review their life experiences, and share those experiences for useful, creative purposes" (p. 15). Gillis and Wagner found that:

> The primary benefits of Life-Writing are those of enabling people to chart their development, the interesting events in their lives, and to write about selected events with some degree of skill and care. The benefits would appear to be obvious in both psychological health and in retaining or developing writing skills and skills of memory perhaps infrequently used. (p. 15)

In conclusion, Gillis and Wagner state:

> In a myriad of ways, Life-Writing for Life-Living seems to be a humanistic project. Almost without conscious planning, it investigates history and culture and is a rich source of oral history. It is aimed to evoke, analyze and recapture the human experience; and to present the results of that process in the enduring forms of imaginative art—poetry, fiction, and autobiography. It epitomizes the process of recognizing the value of the single human spirit, and giving some kind of permanence to that spirit. (p. 15)

In its conceptualization, the Life-Writing Project appears to have utilized much of the theoretical work of David Holbrook and James Britton, especially their research with children's writing. Gillis and Wagner (1980) note that "Holbrook suggested that through the fictionalization or narration of experience, writers are able to symbolize problems and concerns that they are not able to articulate consciously" (p. 8). In an earlier work, Holbrook (1967) states that "creativity is a matter of relationship with oneself, that enables one to come to better terms with the outer world....As we grow better able to work with these subjective processes we become better able to deal with the outside world" (p. 2). James Britton (1970), like Holbrook, believed that the act of writing gave structure to experience. In the Life-Writing Project (Gillis and Wagner, 1980), one of the premises was that if elderly people were to write about the events of their lives, they would acquire a clearer perspective and understanding of who they are, an awareness that would lead to a greater sense of self-worth. The results of the project were generally very positive: "The workshop groups tended to become more self-directed over time; participants began to express more interest in writing outside the workshops—letters to family, friends, memoirs, poetry, and as the workshops progressed, people began to express an interest in expanding the workshops to include discussions of and writing about current events and issues" (p. 15). In other words, though the focus of the writing activities was on reminiscence and the sharing of personal history and experiences, the group's interest moved into a larger social domain.

Roy Bentley and Syd Butler (1986, 1988; Butler & Bentley, 1990, 1992, 1997) spent much of their careers exploring the value of writing workshops, and what they called "lifewriting." In their conceptualization, writers use experience from their lives to center the writing. In this sense, lifewriting is a form of written narration that focuses on the self as a means to conceptualize the self and establish the self's relationship with the outside world. Lifewriting can be defined "as a generic term for all forms of biographic writing" that "provides a large umbrella under which writers, both experts and beginners, can experiment with the expression of their ideas, experiences, and perceptions" (Butler & Bentley, 1992, p. 33).

Lifewriting allows writers to use personal memory and experience to generate text that has significance to them to explore a sense of self. The writing that involves the self as part of the text can include the more accepted, conventional forms of genre such as biography, life stories, and autobiography, but also memoirs, portraits, reminiscences, anecdotes, family histories, dream descriptions, memories, letters, or even oral transcripts. Within this theoretical framework, lifewriting can be considered as an heuristic, or a tool, which can conceptualize the self, and help define the relationship of the self to the outside world at a specific moment in time and space. In this sense, writing is used to "fix" the self at a specific standpoint in life. Because of the importance of lifewriting to the writer, Butler and Bentley saw lifewriting as a means for writers to develop writing abilities and literacy skills.

One of Butler's first attempts at utilizing lifewriting in a writing workshop was a course entitled "Writing for Posterity" which he offered at Brock House, "a social and recreational centre for senior citizens in Vancouver, Canada, with the aim of helping the participants to write stories from their own lives" (Butler, 1985, p. 234). He ran the writing group as a support group with his role "more in the nature of a co-operating editor rather than as an instructor" though he introduced several writing heuristics (p. 236). According to Butler, the group succeeded because the class "encouraged the participants to search their memories for their experience" and provided "a forum for discussion about writing and the sharing of the results" (p. 239). The class helped members to improve their writing, and in the end, they were determined to continue and function "as an autonomous group, with the ability to become self-sustaining, to expand its activities and to provide leadership for other similar groups" (p. 239). The success of the first writing workshop at Brock House can be measured by its continued existence. As of 1999, Butler was still involved with Brock House, which he refers to as "the home of lifewriting" (Butler, 1999, p. 22).

Bentley and Butler (1988) define lifewriting as "the putting down on paper of memories, experiences, and thoughts about one's life or even just about an event in that life. At one level, it is the writing of an autobiography; at the other, it is the capturing of a wisp of a memory in three or four lines of prose or poetry" (p. 7). They found that lifewriting could "deal with the motivations and reactions to present living, or with possible, probable, and even fantastic futures" (p. 7). As well, though writing is usually considered to be a private and solitary activity, they found that the lifewriting workshops were also "a social activity which involve[d] working with other people, talking about experiences and sharing reactions" (p. 7). This social process "serves to stimulate and keep the writer going in capturing these memories" and the "group work becomes not only an important social and therapeutic occasion but also helps the forming and rehearsing in the writers' minds of what they will put down on paper" (p. 7).

Bentley and Butler conduct the writing sessions as writing workshops "which are intrinsic to lifewriting" because the "process that goes on in and around the workshop is every bit as important as the writing product that emerges" (p. 16). Bentley and Butler (1988) state that:

> Even for those who prefer to work privately at getting words on paper, the workshop becomes an enabling structure, a place to get the creative juices going and a place to keep them flowing. It stimulates ideas and the desire to write; it helps not only in coping with, and even conquering, writer's block but also in regulating the actual writing, by forcing the participants to produce, and to produce regularly, not just when "inspiration" comes. The workshop works because it provides a social context. (p. 9)

The social aspect of the writing group is vital because it provides the supportive structure that enables the writing to take place.

Bentley and Butler do not specifically examine or articulate the theoretical underpinnings of the original organization of the lifewriting workshops, but it seems apparent that the ideas of James Britton are extremely relevant. In his three function categories of writing, Britton believed that expressive writing—writing that is close to the self—is "a kind of matrix from which differentiated forms of mature writing are developed" (Britton et al., 1975, p. 83). Emig's concept of reflexive writing covers similar theoretical ground. Lifewriting can be seen as a practical pedagogical application of expressive writing. Expressive writing and lifewriting were important concepts in exploring the value and meaning of the act of writing for the participants of the Writers' Group. In many ways these writers created, or negotiated, a sense of self as a narrative construction utilizing language and text within a series of diverse social and cultural contexts. My work with the Writers' Group looks at the importance of content for individual writers, and how they address issues of race, power, politics, gender and authority through personal writing. Personal writing is always social, and the social is always a consequence of the personal. The personal and social always exist together relationally; one informs the other, and each makes incremental shifts and changes in the other. And it is narrative that weaves the personal and social together in a meaningful pattern.

Chapter Three

Narrative as Knowing, Evocation, and Being

In *Actual Minds, Possible Worlds*, Bruner (1986) maintains that "there are two modes of cognitive functioning, two modes of thought, each providing distinctive ways of ordering experience, of constructing reality" (p. 11). The paradigmatic, or logico-scientific mode, represents the dominant language of science, business, and modern communication, and "attempts to fulfill the ideal of a formal, mathematical system of description and explanation" (p. 12). Much of the theoretical work in writing functions in the paradigmatic mode. Bruner suggests that the "imaginative application of the paradigmatic mode" of thinking leads to "good theory, tight analysis, logical proof, sound argument, and empirical discovery guided by reasoned hypothesis" (p. 13).

The other mode of cognitive thinking as a way of knowing is narrative, which focuses not on the development of a well-formed argument, but instead on the creation of a good, believable story. Bruner claims "the two (though complementary) are irreducible to one another. Efforts to reduce one mode to the other or to ignore one at the expense of the other inevitably fail to capture the rich diversity of thought" (p. 11). In many ways, writing theorists and educators have focused on the first mode of cognitive thinking, the paradigmatic, and ignored the second mode, the narrative. Yet, it is possible that humans, for the most part, conceptualize the world and their reality through the construction of story. Narrative organizes experience into sequential and relational patterns as a way of knowing. If it is true that we know the world narratively, then we need to reexamine the value of writing in curriculum theory and design.

Narrative, therefore, becomes a way of seeing not only the experiences of the Writers' Group participants, but a way of seeing writing process theory. This book is not only a study of writing, but also a study of people who write. If Bruner is correct in his declaration that people understand the world through story, then narrative gives us a different insight into the lives of the participants of the Writers' Group, and the value that writing has in their lives. The writers at CMHA value writing in ways that are different from what the academic community has usually validated. Writing for them, in many cases, becomes an act of community and a means to gain perspective and a measure of control over life's experience. In this book, the focus is on individuals, and the value they assign to their work, and in doing so reflects some of the value that Holbrook (1964, 1967, 1979) and Macrorie (1970, 1974, 1988) espoused in their work in validating the individual within the larger social context.

As it stands, the theory of writing process is often seen by many researchers as a logical developmental process conceived in the paradigmatic mode. Revisiting writing process theory from a narrative perspective, including the concepts developed by Paul Ricoeur (1984) has potential to open up a deeper discussion. As Bruner has noted, "the ways of telling and the ways of conceptualizing that go with them become so habitual that they finally become recipes for structuring experience itself" (Bruner, 1988, p. 582). The way of seeing the world becomes the way of understanding the world, which becomes the way to represent the world.

I am using narrative as a central construct for this book, linking story and context in connection with logic and reason to provide a new perspective on what it means to write. In doing so, I am considering, and utilizing, the concept of narrative in three different ways to thoroughly explore the experiences of the writers. One, I am using narrative as a way of knowing and seeing the world in a holistic and relational manner. Bruner (1986) proposed that humans utilize two ways of knowing. Narrative looks at the world in a holistic sense, making sense of phenomena and events by creating story. Paradigmatic knowing is logical, rational, and based on analysis. In this book, I weave narrative knowing together with paradigmatic knowing to create a deeper sense of meaning.

Two, I am using narrative as a literary structure to render, or evoke, the experiences of the writers involved in the Writers' Group. This mode of narrative is based on living the life of an artist and seeing the world in relational patterns, and evoking this vision of the stories we live and imagine.

Three, I am considering narrative as one of the fundamental ways in which humans construct a sense of who they are in relation to the world, and as a means of constructing reality. This third mode of narrative is central to an understanding of the value these writers ascribe to their writing, and how they each create a sense of self through the stories they tell.

In this book, I want to understand and evoke the experiences of the participants of the CMHA Writers' Group contextually to reconsider writing theory and what it means to write. Rather than simply analyzing their writing and experiences from a paradigmatic, or logico-scientific, focus, I looked at the writers in terms of an inter-textual story. Another reason I used a narrative lens to conduct the study is to look at how writers compose from a story or contextual point of view. Researchers, for the most part, have looked at how writers compose from a cognitive point of view. Flower and Hayes (1981) attempted to understand the linear, sequential movement of idea to a finished piece of writing. Even Britton, with his often radical perspectives on composition, usually used a paradigmatic lens to see his ideas and concepts.

One of the dominant objectives with this book was to explore the complexity of the relationships involved in the Writers' Group, and the act of writing both as an individual act and as a social construction. Writing does not occur in isolation. As Perry (2000) has noted: "Writing knowledge, 'knowing how' to write, cannot be separated from the 'knowing what' and 'knowing that' of writing" (p. 206). Narrative inquiry provides a valuable framework for the examination of the value of personal writing because it "organizes human experiences into temporally meaningful episodes" and is "the primary form by which human experience is made meaningful" (Polkinghorne, 1988, p. 1). I am very concerned with how to construct meaning from the experience of the CMHA Writers' Group, and how to represent that meaning for the reader. In evoking the experiences of the writers, I used narrative as "a meaning structure that organizes events and human actions into a whole" (Polkinghorne, 1988, p. 18). I wanted the experiences of the writers to be central to an understanding of what it means to write.

The use of story or narrative as a means of seeing and understanding the world is certainly not new. Novelists and artists have been aware of it, and have actively pursued it, for centuries. Novels often become central to our way of knowing, or seeing, a specific world. As an example, the novels of Tolstoy and Dostoyevsky provide an insight into Russian life in ways that science, economics, or conventional history cannot.

In 1890, William James wrote:

> To say that all human thinking is essentially of two kinds—reasoning on the one hand, and narrative, descriptive, contemplative thinking on the other—is to say that every reader's experience will corroborate. (quoted in Bruner, 1986, frontispiece)

William James was simply summarizing what writers and artists have always known. Narrative is another way of thinking of the world, and thereby knowing the world. In many ways, we "know" the world through story. In creating the narratives of the four writers (see Chapter Four), I am inviting the reader to know the world of these writers through narrative.

A writer or artist is more concerned with believability and the understanding of a truth than the knowing of a static truth that can be measured precisely. Picasso (1972) stated, "We all know that Art is not truth. Art is a lie that makes us realize the truth" (p. 21). Narrative does not pretend to reveal a concrete and hegemonic truth. Narrative is a way of understanding "lived experience" because we locate "narrative in human actions and the events which surround them, and in our capacity to perceive the world as consisting of...actions, and events sequentially ordered" (Rosen, 1987, p. 13).

In the social and human sciences, narrative inquiry has become a more popular research methodology in recent years. Narrative as a way of knowing and understanding, and as a way of representing lived experience, offers an alternative to a positivistic model of research. Clandinin and Connelly (1996, 2000; Connelly & Clandinin, 1999), two prominent narrative methodologists, contend:

> With narrative as our vantage point, we have a point of reference, a life and a ground to stand on for imagining what experience is and for imagining how it might be studied and represented in researchers' texts. In this view, experience is the stories people live. (Clandinin & Connelly, 1994, cited in 2000, p. xxvi)

Narrative is a reconstruction of a lived experience told in carefully delineated and contextual frames. As John Dewey noted, "experience is both social and personal...and [people] are always in relation" (cited in Clandinin & Connelly, 2000, p. 2). Reality, as seen from this perspective, becomes a complex social construction. Instead of searching for truth, narrative is an extremely valuable heuristic for gaining an insight and understanding of a specific experience and how humans construct meaning. The American author Paul Auster suggests, "We construct a narrative for ourselves and that's the thread we follow from one day to the next. People who disintegrate as personalities are the ones who lose that thread" (cited in Fulford, 1999, p. 13). Narrative in many ways creates, or constructs, the self; we are the summation of our stories. Robert Fulford (1999) notes that:

> narrative, as opposed to analysis, has the power to mimic the unfolding of reality. Narrative is selective and maybe untrue, but it can produce the feeling of events occurring in time; it seems to be rooted in reality. This is also the reason for the triumph of narrative, its penetration and in some ways its dominance of our collective imagination; with a combination of ancient devices and up-to-the minute technology, it can appear to replicate life. (p. 16)

Narrative, in this sense, evokes the experience of being in the world, and a means to convey experience to others.

In my study of the CMHA Writers' Group, I was concerned with seeing the experiences of the writers narratively, as well as conveying and representing those experiences and stories in such a way that the world of the writers would be evoked within the reader. It is the ability of narrative to replicate life that is both its great advantage over positivistic models, and the source of some of its greatest criticism. Barone and Eisner (1997), in their article on art-based education research, introduce the importance of empathic understanding:

> The ability to understand empathically is the ability to participate vicariously in another form of life. With the arts and humanities, empathic understanding is the result of an inquirer's achievement of intersubjectivity. The inquirer's use of contextualized, expressive, and vernacular language motivates the readers to reconstruct the subjects' perspective within themselves. Second, empathic understanding is the inquirer's ability to promote the reconstruction of that perspective within her or his readers. (p. 77)

Narrative does not try to mirror reality; it tries to replicate lived experience. Literary language is especially powerful because it "allows re-creation of the mental atmosphere, feelings, and motivations of the characters in a story, drama, or essay" (Barone & Eisner, 1997, p. 77). Literary language in narrative can allow the reader's entrance into the lived experience and thereby create a deeper understanding of a specific world, at a specific point in time.

Anthropologist Stephen Tyler (1986) has attempted to explain the complexity of representation in post-modern ethnography:

> Because its meaning is not in it but in an understanding, of which it is only a consumed fragment, it is no longer cursed with the task of representation. The key word in understanding this difference is "evoke," for if a discourse can be said to "evoke," then it need not represent what it evokes, though it may be a means to a representation. Since evocation is nonrepresentational, it is not to be understood as a sign function, for it is not a "symbol of", not does it "symbolize" what it evokes. (p. 129)

Ellis (1997) also uses the concept of evocation in her research methodology, and is "less concerned with 'historical truth' and more involved with 'narrative truth'" (p. 128). Ellis will often "condense a number of scenes into evocative composites" instead of trying to create a "mirror representation of chronologically ordered events" (p. 128). In doing so, she would create a story, "where the events and feelings cohered, and where readers could grasp the main points and feel some of what [she] felt" (p. 128). Since I am concerned with the reader understanding what occurs at the Writers' Group, the narratives I created are *evocative* rather than *representational*.

Lincoln (1995) suggested that "attention to voice—to who speaks, for whom, to whom, for what purpose—effectively creates praxis, even when no praxis was intended" (p. 282). Voice, "as resistance against silence, as resistance to disengagement, as resistance to marginalization," is a necessary component of "passionate participation" (p. 282). Voice is central to interpretive work, and "the extent to which alternative voices are heard is a criterion by which we can judge the openness, engagement, and problematic nature of any text" (p. 283). Yet voice is an exceedingly complex concept in writing, and in research methodology. It is often assumed that voice is the exact correspondence of the writing style and content with the writer's actual, inner self. This assumption, though common in writing-process theory, is far too simplistic. Leggo (1989), in his doctoral dissertation entitled *Search(ing) (For) Voices(s)*, thoroughly explored voice, yet at the end admits he does not really know exactly what voice is. This confession is by no means a defeat; it is simply an acknowledgment of the complexity of voice. The authenticity of voice, and authentic representation or evocation of voice, are very serious concerns in social research. Admittedly, there are no easy solutions. A researcher needs to be diligent, honest, and constantly in a state of what Clandinin and Connelly (2000) call "wakefulness," a constant process of reflection. It is worthwhile to quote at length from Clandinin and Connelly (2000) about a researcher's difficulty in creating a research text using voice:

> One of the researcher's dilemmas in the composing of research texts is captured by the analogy of living on an edge, trying to maintain one's balance, as one struggles to express one's own voice in the midst of an inquiry designed to tell of the participants' storied experiences and to represent their voices, all the while attempting to create a research text that will speak to, and reflect upon, the audience's voices. Voice, and dilemmas created by the consideration of it, are always sorted out by the exercise of judgment.
>
> One key consideration is the multiplicity of voices both for participants and for researchers. We need not to see our participants as univocal, not tied to one theoretical structure or mode of behavior that would leave them with the appearance of being unidimensional. We, and our participants, live and tell many stories. We are all characters with multiple plotlines who speak from within these multiple plotlines....As researchers, we too struggle to speak our research texts in our multiple voices. Our silences, both those we choose and those of which we are unaware, are also considerations of voice in our research texts. (p. 147)

I have considered the multiplicity of voice, weaving the stories of the writer participants with mine to create a narrative thread that gives an insight into what happens at the Writers' Group, and why the writing is so valuable and important to the participating writers. I created narratives that give voice to the individual writers. In many ways, the resulting narratives were co-creations with the writers who are involved because I was able to use the writers' own words and writing to illustrate themes and ideas. I have used voice as a construct to evoke the experience, and not as a simple representation of reality.

In narrative inquiry, the context and relationships of the participants are essential to the understanding of any social phenomenon. A researcher is within the phenomenon, not outside, looking in. Clandinin and Connelly (2000) suggest that narrative inquiries "continually negotiate their relationships" with the participants, and that these "relationships need to be 'worked at'" (p. 73). This negotiation is essential in a narrative inquiry if one is willing to acknowledge the complexity of social phenomena. Kincheloe (1991) suggests that:

> A postmodern mode of analysis assumes that the world is complex, characterized by a web-like configuration of interacting forces. Scientists, like everyone else are inside, not outside, the web...the knower and the known are inseparable—they are both a part of the web of reality. No one in this web-like configuration of the universe can achieve a God-like perspective—no one can totally escape the web and look back at it from afar. We all must confess our subjectivity; we must recognize our limited vantage point. To recognize how our particular view of the web shapes our conception of educational reality, we need to understand our historicity. (p. 119)

In an attempt to be constantly vigilant of the historicity, I was in constant contact with the four participants during the writing of this book. Often they would telephone or e-mail me to clarify points or issues that were raised in conversation, the writing sessions, and personal interviews. We were all together, knower and known, all part of the web of reality.

I embedded the narrators' stories and historicities in a relational, contextual framework within the theoretical and analytical components of writing theory. Kincheloe (1991) notes that:

> Cause-effect educational research tends to ignore the way our historicity (our place in space and time) works to construct our consciousness; as a result, our concept of social activity and of the educational process is reduced to a static frame. Thus, the positivistic researcher feels empowered to make predictions, to settle questions, to ignore the dialectical process in which all social activity is grounded. (p. 119)

Without a "dialectical process" between researcher and participant, the narratives become extraneous data. I do not view narratives as anecdotal stories that can then be used as commodities that exist separately from the lived experiences of the participants. Stories are not to be used as building blocks to support theories that are imposed on phenomena. Stories are an integral part of the participants' lived experiences and cannot be appropriated from the narrators.

I constantly employed member checks as a means of avoiding any problems and issues. All writing pertaining to the participants was shared with them to ensure accuracy and complete agreement.

The negotiation of relationships is not limited by the researcher's connection with participants. There is also a constant negotiation of the researcher's positionality in what Clandinin and Connelly (2000) call the "three-dimensional narrative inquiry space" in dealing with the lived experience of others:

> With this sense of Dewey's foundational place [Dewey's theory of experience, and his notions of situation, continuity, and interaction] in our thinking about narrative inquiry, our terms are personal, and social (interaction); past, present, and future (continuity); combined with the notion of place (situation). This set of terms creates a metaphorical *three-dimensional narrative inquiry space*, with temporality along one dimension, the personal and the social along a second dimension, and place along a third. Using this set of terms, any particular inquiry is defined by this three-dimensional space: studies have temporal dimensions and address temporal matters; they focus on the personal and the social in a balance appropriate to the inquiry; and they occur in specific places or sequences of places. (p. 50)

As a researcher and writer, I tried to pay constant attention to my positionality and historicity within the three-dimensional narrative inquiry space, especially in the relationship of my field notes and research text. Without a clear explication of context, stories based on the interview transcripts and memory become "unnuanced facts" that cannot be resolved with the final text (Clandinin & Connelly, 2000, p. 141). Lincoln (1995) addresses this issue in her article "Emerging Criteria for Quality in Qualitative and Interpretive Research":

> Positionality, or standpoint epistemology, recognizes the poststructural, postmodern argument that texts, any texts, are always partial and incomplete; socially, culturally, historically, racially, and sexually located; and can therefore never represent any truth except those truths that exhibit the same characteristics....For standpoint epistemologists, only texts that display their own contextual grounds for argumentation would be eligible for appellations of quality and rigor. (p. 280)

I was very conscious of the complexity of the relationships within the social sphere of the Writers' Group and strived to maintain an openness, both to the Writers' Group and the reader, that acknowledged that the narratives and resulting analyses were always filtered through my positionality in the group and the study.

Barone and Eisner (1997; Barone et al., 1999) suggest using arts-based research as another alternative that utilizes writing as an inquiry method. Eisner has argued at recent American Educational Research Association conferences that novels should be accepted as legitimate dissertations in educational research

(Barone et al., 1999). Barone and Eisner (1997) suggest that each arts-based literary inquiry would embody "the unique vision of its author" and provide a "personal statement arising out of the negotiations between an author and the phenomena under scrutiny" (p. 78). The reader would be invited to enter a "virtual reality" (p. 73) to gain a new meaning of the phenomenon under study.

In this book, I used my own writing as a form of research inquiry, with narrative, or story, as the organizing methodology. This methodology allowed me to acknowledge the complexity of subjectivity, inter-textuality, and multiple voices in a research inquiry. The use of narrative acknowledges that the language itself is a part of the structure of the study. Ellis and Bochner (2000) state that "language is not transparent and there's no single standard of truth...validity means that our work seeks verisimilitude; it evokes in readers a feeling that the experience described is lifelike, believable, and possible" (p. 751). I had a commitment to understanding the experiences of the participants of the Writers' Group, and then evoking in the reader what occurs at the CMHA Writers' Group as accurately and with as much verisimilitude as possible, utilizing the voices of the participants as well as embedding my own subjectivity into the analysis of the phenomenon.

Another option for narrative inquiry I employed in this study was to use the writing itself as a research tool. Richardson (2000) states that "writing is also a way of 'knowing'—a method of discovery and analysis. By writing in different ways, we discover new aspects of our topic and our relationship to it. Form and content are inseparable" (p. 923). Her statement echoes the ideas of the poet Allen Ginsberg who believed that content always creates its own form (personal communication, September 28, 1987).

The idea of using writing as a research inquiry extends writing-process theory based on writing to learn, writing across the curriculum, and Macrorie's (1988) work with I-Search papers. Coles (1988), in *The Plural I and After*, wrote:

> I value writing...as a uniquely powerful instrument for learning, as a special way of thinking and coming to know. I value it as a form of language...as the primary means by which all of us run orders through chaos thereby giving ourselves the identities we have. (p. 285)

Writing can easily be seen as a way of knowing which considers the centrality of language to our sense of identity. White and Hellerich (1998) state that:

> Language, including the entire realm of semiotic practices—from words to gestures to video images and music—is, as Lacan has argued, the domain in which the self is constructed. For subjectivity is created by self-reference, in Lacan's view, by the

> identification of self with an external, mirror image and the introjection of that image as the personality. (p. 2)

In my research and in the creation of this book, the writing itself became the meaning-making site of the research inquiry, since "language does not 'reflect' social reality, but produces meaning, creates social reality" (Richardson, 2000, p. 928). Carlos Fuentes (1985) writes "nothing is seen until the writer names it. Language permits us to see. Without the word, we are all blind" (p. 146). In this sense, I am using language as a lens for the reader to 'see' the world of the writers who attend the CMHA Writers' Group, and through a narrative evocation, perhaps create a means for the reader to enter that world.

The writing becomes a way of knowing, and a way of being. Bruner has recently expanded his ideas of narrative as a way of knowing, to consider narrative as a central means of how humans construct a sense of self. In "Life as Narrative" (1987) and "The Narrative Construal of Reality" (1996) Bruner examines narrative as a fundamental way in which humans construct a life. Narrative, when considered from this perspective is not just a way of knowing, but a way of being. This is similar to Turner's (1996) concept of the "literary mind" which he maintains "is not a separate kind of mind. It is our mind. The literary mind is the fundamental mind" (preface). Turner maintains, "Story is a basic principle of mind. Most of our experience, our knowledge and our thinking is organized as stories" (preface). This idea of narrative is important to consider. Turner claims:

> Narrative imagining—story—is the fundamental instrument of thought. Rational capacities depend upon it. It is our chief means of looking into the future, of predicting, of planning, and of explaining. It is a literary capacity indispensable to human cognition generally. (p. 5)

These ideas of narrative have greatly influenced my thinking, in the exploration of the value of writing, and the construction of this book. Narrative becomes a way of knowing, a way of evoking experience and finally, a way of being.

In the next chapter I introduce the reader to the four writers from Writers' Group and provide some relational context for the narratives of four of the main participants in my research project. I do not see myself as a researcher gazing into the Writers' Group and objectively measuring what the experience is like for the participants. Instead, I am an active participant who has the added responsibility of organizing the group and creating a safe environment for the members to attend and participate without fear or apprehension. I write when they write; I actively participate in the discussions. I don't see the Writers' Group as an artifact that needs to be measured or represented. I think of the Writers' Group as a living event. I do not pretend to be an objective researcher. The line between object and subject is blurred. For some readers this may cloud the validity; for other readers, this blurring of vision may ironically provide greater clarity in understanding the experience of these writers. Ellis and Flaherty (1992) suggest that researchers:

> return from their explorations with descriptions and interpretations intended "to keep a conversation going" (Rorty 1979). Ultimately, it is a conversation through which we can come to know ourselves and others and the positions from which we speak; a conversation that unites the humanities and the sciences. (pp. 5-6)

It was my intent to actively engage in the conversations involving writing theory. Narratives are always created in an historical, cultural, and social context; therefore, in order to understand the story, one must understand the context of this study.

I cite an anecdote concerning the French psychoanalyst, Jacques Lacan, to provide an illustration of the complexity of relationships and vision:

> Years ago when [Lacan] was fishing off Brittany, a friend pointed to a sardine can in the water and said laughingly, "You see that can. Do you see it? Well, it doesn't see you!" Ruminating on the lesson his friend had drawn from the floating can, Lacan concluded that it was mistaken, for the can "was looking at me, all the same. It was looking at me at the level of the point of light, the point of light, the point at which everything that looks at me is situated—and I am not speaking metaphorically." Lacan, in other words, felt that he was indeed in the center of a conflictual visual field, at once the eye looking at the can and the screen in an impersonal field of pure monstrance. His subjectivity was thus split between the apex at the end of the triangle of the eye and the line in the middle of the triangle of the gaze. He was both the viewer of Holbein's painting and the smeared skull in its visual field. (Jay, 1993, pp. 365-366)

This quotation reaffirms the complexity of the issues of representing the world of the researcher and the research participants. I am part of this study, both as an active participant of the Writers' Group, and as a researcher trying to gain an understanding into the nature of writing. As well, as the writer of this study, I created voice for both the participants and myself by providing a narrative context for the research that is always contextualized within the relationships of all the participants, including myself.

In the following chapter, the reader is invited to read the four narratives of the writers as integrated research. The narratives are not to be read as appendixes, or as background stories. In many ways, the narratives are the heart of the book because they evoke the experiences of the writers and the importance of writing in their lives—they are writers at work in the riparian zone, constantly negotiating meaning and significance in their lives.

Part II

The Riparian Zone

"If only we could find a pure, reserved, narrow bit of the human, our own strip of fertile land between river and rock. For our heart still overreaches us, just as theirs did them. And no longer can we gaze back after it in images, which calm it, or in godlike bodies where more grandly it tempers itself."

Rainer Maria Rilke,
Second Elegy, The Duino Elegies

Chapter Four

Narratives as Integrated Research

"The universe is made of stories, not atoms."
Muriel Rukeyser

In this book I have interwoven narrative and paradigmatic writing together, for a number of reasons. The paradigmatic writing was valuable in providing a scholarly context and an analysis for research; the narrative writing was important in providing a central space for the participants' voices in the book, and to evoke the experience of what occurs at the Writers' Group. Overall, I have created a narrative in which I present the stories of several participants, and make meaning or significance both in their own right as narratives, and through the lens of the conceptual framework outlined in this study.

The four narratives of participants from the CMHA Writers' Group are not simply a summation of research data. The narratives are meant to evoke the worlds of the writers, and when read in conjunction with the paradigmatic strands of the book, create a deeper meaning and understanding for the reader.

It is usual in a research project to use pseudonyms to protect the anonymity and confidentiality of the participants. Caroline Murphy and Warren McDonald are pseudonyms; however, Brian Borley and Albert Chatsis requested that their real names be used in the study. To protect the identities of Caroline and Warren, I have slightly altered specific details of their narratives.

I met with Brian Borley after the interviews to get him to sign his release of transcript and writing data, and explained the usual research protocol of using pseudonyms. At that time, he said he would agree to whatever I wanted for the research regarding the use of names, saying that he understood the need to protect the participants, but that he would rather have his real name used in the study. "I mean, Jeff, I have my own Web page. If someone cares enough to figure out who I am, it wouldn't be that hard. I want people to learn more about mental health, and to understand that we are real people too. I have published lots of letters in the paper and magazines. I have no problem with people knowing that I'm mentally ill. I know that your university would rather have the study anonymous. If that has to be, I'm okay with that too. I just think the research is important. You can do whatever you feel is right."

My encounters with Albert were equally enlightening to me because it really drove home the balance we must keep as researchers. When I explained the usual protocol of using pseudonyms for research studies in social sciences, he became upset and puzzled. "They are my stories and I told them as honestly as possible. I want you to use my real name. If you don't, it isn't honest." I explained that the use of pseudonyms was designed to protect him by not revealing his name and mental condition, and his association with a mental health organization. "I still want my real name used. If you put someone else's name on it, it isn't me. I want to be known for who I am."

I eventually wrote another waiver form and had Brian and Albert sign a letter of release from the use of pseudonyms in the research study. The demarcation line between researcher and research participant was blurred right from the beginning of this study. The research project was a voyage of discovery and understanding for all of us, with the participants functioning as active constructors of meaning—of their own experience and their perceptions of the experience of the Writers' Group.

All the narratives, although heavily based on interview transcripts and conversations recorded in my journal notations, are in some way literary constructions. In creating the narratives, I agree with Barone (1990) when he suggests that "the primary form of written narrative discourse—and therefore of qualitative texts about human experience—is literature" (p. 306). The narratives are also a continuation of Bruner's (1986) two ways of knowing, and provide an alternative vision into the meaning of the Writers' Group from somewhere other than a paradigmatic, logico-scientific perspective.

In creating the narratives, I first conducted a series of in-depth interviews with four writers from the Writers' Group. I used purposeful sampling (Lincoln & Guba, 1985; Merriam, 1998) to select the participants, based on such criteria as longevity in the Writers' Group and interest in the act of writing.

I modeled the interview style on the work of Seidman (1998), who uses in-depth interviews from a phenomenological approach, trying to reach an understanding of the point of view of the interview participant. The interviews were designed in a three-part framework. Each part of the interviewing process was approximately ninety minutes in length, though the time was always negotiable with the participants. The first interview tried to ground the context of the participant and create a miniature life story. The second interview looked at the experience of the Writers' Group, while the third interview focused on how the participant made sense of the act of writing, as well as the experience of belonging to a writing group. At all times I encouraged the participants to engage in an open discussion of why they found writing important in their lives, and to explore the social aspect of the Writers' Group. According to Seidman, people's experience and behavior become "meaningful and understandable when placed in the contexts of their lives and the lives or those around them" (1998, p. 11).

I found Seidman's interview structure extremely valuable, although I had some concerns with his approach. In his interpretation of phenomenology, he assumes that it is possible to understand the "lived experience" of another being through observation, clear interview techniques and data analysis. Another assumption is that the respondent is constant over time and space. I have doubts about this. Consequently, I believe that there is much merit in the work of Holstein and Gubrium (1995, 1997) with "active interviewing" which "brings meaning and its construction to the foreground" (Holstein & Gubrium, 1995, p. 73). Their work anticipates, in many ways, the complexity of voice in a research inquiry. Holstein and Gubrium (1995) note that "the subject behind the respondent may change virtually from comment to comment" (p. 74).

Holstein and Gubrium's work with active interviewing suggests that neither the subject nor the phenomenon is completely fixed. It might therefore be impossible to measure, or even to understand, a phenomenon or subject completely. Perhaps the best a researcher can accomplish is to create an agreed-upon meaning, acknowledging the subjectivity of the researcher, and the shifting subject behind the respondent, while looking at a phenomenon that also may change as it is being studied. This might best be referred to as the social sciences' acknowledgment of Heisenberg's Uncertainty Principle. In this perspective, the research inquiry becomes a shifting dance of the phenomenon, the participants and the researcher.

Using a combination of Seidman's phenomenological in-depth interviews, tempered with Holstein and Gubrium's active interviews, I was able to gain a deep understanding of what writing and the writing group experience meant to the participants in this study.

I tape-recorded all the interviews, and transcribed them myself. The participants read over the transcripts to verify their literal accuracy, and had input into their final shape. After consulting with the individuals involved I retyped the transcripts with their corrections and clarifications. For the most part they accepted the transcripts with few corrections.

Since the beginning of my involvement with the Writers' Group over ten years ago, I have actively been involved in all the writing sessions, writing while the rest of the group wrote. For this research project, I shifted from writing more creative pieces to writing field notes and reflexive journal entries during the writing sessions. The other change in my usual weekly routine with the group was that I rarely read my writing aloud as I normally would. I did this to protect the participants and not to interfere with the usual routine of the Writers' Group. I created "thick description" to describe the research site, the participants, and the writing environment. I kept a reflexive journal to record my own feelings and responses to the research. I think that the descriptive field notes, coupled with the reflexive journal, allowed me to contextualize myself in the research, acknowledge my historicity and monitor and negotiate my relationship with the participants.

Because of the complexity of voice and positionality in this study, I utilized what Denzin (1997) labels reflexive, "messy texts" in my field notes and reflexive journals, which often acted as a site of meaning negotiation. Denzin suggests that:

> criticisms [of naturalism and its presumed connection between lived experience and the written word] open the door for the reflexive, messy text: texts that are aware of their own narrative apparatuses, that are sensitive to how reality is socially constructed, and that...writing is a way of "framing" reality. Messy texts are many sited, intertextual, always open ended, and resistant to theoretical holism, but always committed to cultural criticism. (p. 224)

The use of the reflexive, "messy texts" allowed for the multiplicity of voice that I wished to achieve in my research. They also allowed me to embed my subjectivity and historicity in the study. Denzin further suggests that messy texts:

> move back and forth between description, interpretation, and voice. These texts erase the dividing line between observer and observed. In them, the writer is transformed into a scribe who writes for rather than about the individuals being studied...Still, these texts make the writer's experiences central to the topic at hand. The messy text produces local, situated knowledge about the practices of a given group and its culture. There is always a stress on the historical contingencies and social processes that shape and play on the situations and persons under study. The messy text re-creates a social world as a site at which identities and local cultures are negotiated and given meaning. (p. 225)

The use of reflexive texts, which acknowledge the subjectivity of the inquirer as well as the central importance of the participants as meaning-makers, had great significance in this research project. I was able to create meaning by combining my own subjectivity and lived experience, which were constantly enveloped by the scholarly and theoretical context, with the lived experiences of the Writers' Group participants. This multiplicity allowed me to represent the experiences of the Writers' Group participants with a narrative depth.

The narratives I created evoke the experience of the writers, but do not presume to represent an objective reality. As Barone (1990) states:

> In this reordering, elements of experience are recast into a form that is analogous to but does not replicate an actual experience. A work of art, says Langer (1957), is a semblance, a composed apparition. In experiencing this semblance the reader lives vicariously in a virtual world, only temporarily bracketed off from the mundane, the nearby. What he experiences there is an idea of subjective life. In this reconstructive process, I mean, the self of the reader discovers an "otherness" (Poulet, 1986). Awareness arises of an alternate consciousness, a "mind" behind the effect, a fellow being responsible for the virtual event now formally re-created. The reader hears the voice of another subject offering the fruits of her inquiry into the qualities of lived experience. (p. 307)

The narratives of the four writers provide a literary construction of what occurs at the Writers' Group, and what sense or understanding the participants make of their experiences. The evocation is important because it replicates the experiences of the writers, and provides a context for the writing and theoretical analysis which occur later in the book.

Each of these individual narratives is constructed uniquely, and each functions in slightly different ways from the others. The four narratives interweave like a sonata (Sconiers & Rosiek, 2000), each story adding a slightly different perspective of how the participants of the CMHA Writers' Group value writing.

The narratives are integral to a full understanding of what occurs at the Writers' Group, and what meaning the individual writers ascribe to the act of writing. The individual narratives can be read as part of the exploration into compositional theory, and are not meant to simply add color, or detail. I wanted the narrative way of knowing to be fully integrated with the paradigmatic analysis offered later in the book. It is only in that paradoxical space between "narrative knowing" and "paradigmatic knowing" that a deeper meaning can be contextualized.

Brian Borley

Brian Borley is a sixty-seven-year-old former teacher who has attended the Writers' Group for the last eight years. He is a very enthusiastic and prodigious writer who rarely misses the weekly writing sessions; he also completes a great deal of writing at home. Since he has started attending the Writers' Group, Brian has written two novels, has had several letters to the editor published, and has articles on mental health and education published in various magazines. In the last year he has started his own Web page, and has made a lot of his writing available to the public through this medium.

The first-person narrative of Brian Borley is based on a series of in-depth interviews I conducted with him over several months. I also used Brian's e-mail correspondence with me, as well as his writing from the Writers' Group sessions, and various other material he forwarded to me over the years. I created a first-person narrative because it best evokes and re-creates Brian's experience at the Writers' Group, and shows the value that writing has in his life. Brian freely gave his consent, and has checked over this narrative several times to offer comments and suggestions, many of which were incorporated in further revisions. Brian said to me when he had gone over the narrative, "I see what you've done and I'm very happy with it. You've given my words a shape that makes the meaning clearer to the reader. I believe the narrative fits me like a well pressed suit" (personal correspondence and e-mail correspondence).

Brian was extremely active in this research project. I did not simply observe and study him, and I did not interview him from a positivist perspective, or even a strictly phenomenological perspective. Instead, we were looking at issues and ideas and co-constructing a meaning together. The research was very much a dialectic, with the understanding of the value of writing as a dominant focus. This co-construction was evident when Brian e-mailed several times with further writing on subjects we had introduced in the interviews. There were also many times when I telephoned Brian to further clarify an idea or an observation. The meaning was often constructed together as we attempted to understand the value and importance of writing.

Brian's narrative incorporates the original research data of participant observation and the interviews, along with my resulting e-mail correspondence with him. He clarified some statements and changed some of the pronoun usage that in the interview transcripts had occasionally shifted from first to second person. This shifting of pronouns is quite common in oral discourse, but he wanted the pronouns in agreement for the most part. As Brian explained, "The original version probably reflected the way I speak. The edited version reflects the way I write. I still believe I write a good deal better than I talk. I've done some editing of the document in an attempt to provide the language with a better flow. You can be the final judge of that. I believe I have cleaned up the inappropriate use of pronouns. Is there a rule that the subjective pronouns are supposed to be constant within a paragraph? From my days as an English student (a very pedestrian one, I might add, an observation which my school records will attest to), I recall something about this consistency. As far as content and the ideas I have expressed, I am happy with the way they are portrayed" (Brian, e-mail, August 1, 2001).

The Narrative of Brian Borley: Writing Is My Playground

As a writer, I write mostly because I must write. Writing is my playground. Putting words, ideas, and sentences on paper is one of my favorite games. I find it relaxing and entertaining, and I enjoy doing it. It is something I can focus on and play with, and what I love about the Writers' Group is having a community with which to share my writing. As writers, if we want to perfect our skills, we need criticism. The feedback is valuable, both the positive and negative, though it is mostly positive, and it is always honest. It's the feedback, as well as the social aspect of the group, that is important, because it confirms who we are. Writing confirms and strengthens personal identity.

I've been attending the Writers' Group for about seven years. My son Joe and I walk over from our duplex in Westview every Tuesday night. I've been around so long they let me have a key. We like to get there early to set up the tables, and Joe always makes the coffee. People start arriving a little before seven. Sometimes some of the people who take the bus will be waiting outside the door. There used to be a small bench outside the door, but someone stole it last winter.

For many of the people at the Writers' Group, this is the closest thing they have to a home. It is the one constant for them and they know it is always there. It's like that television show, *Cheers*, except we don't have the beer. The Writers' Group is one of the strongest institutions I've ever been involved with, and I really feel good about being part of it. It's a place where people can connect and not be afraid to show a little intimacy, and also not be afraid to preserve a comfortable level of distance at the same time. People can just be.

I come to the Writers' Group because it is one of the high points in my week. The Writers' Group provides an opportunity to socialize in a very safe, comfortable, and supportive setting. I really find it gratifying to see, to witness, the emotional and intellectual growth of everyone there, including myself. I think the writing, in part by accident, focuses or finds its focus in the things that are important to the people who come there. And to be able to share all these features and broaden them, you're building a safer and more comfortable and interesting world.

I would say unequivocally that the Writers' Group, second only from the support I get from my family, has had the greatest single impact on my rehabilitation, and that is saying quite a bit. You see, when you can meet with a group of people who share common concerns, common crises, and share ways in which we can deal with them, and put it in the form of language, we can deal with it. Then we are a really strong growth-inducing organization.

It's a continuing process. The Writers' Group is a place to gain self-awareness. It is a place to share thoughts and feelings and a good measure of intimacy with the members in that group. And all this leads, it seems to me, to personal growth. I mean, you grow as a person. You grow emotionally. You grow intellectually, and have some response to the things that you say. I was mentioning last night that one member, one of my most ardent critics, though not to say that she is critical in a negative sense, is not at all shy about pointing out things she doesn't agree with. When I reflect on what she says and revise my ideas I become better educated. This is part of it, too. It is an ongoing process. I think I will probably be continuing in the group as long as I can walk over.

I think going to the Writers' Group has done wonders for my writing. I believe that there are others, besides myself, who do a lot of writing on their own as well and who probably wouldn't be if they hadn't been motivated by the experience of that Tuesday night group. It's because of the feedback. Without a warm and, in some cases intimate, social interaction, it's not very fulfilling. People enjoy being seen and they enjoy being heard, and they enjoy being recognized for something that they do well. And this builds. There are two interacting things. One is not separate from the other. The social development and the communication development go hand in hand. I mean the communications factor supports the strength of the group socially, and the strength of the group socially improves their communication because it breaks down walls. The two are mutually supportive.

The way the group is run, and the atmosphere, the way we do things is very important and valuable. I could give you a comparison. I was involved in a few group therapy sessions in hospital and so on, where they get people sitting around in a circle. Usually these groups are very much, and subtly, dominated by a leader. Although they are trying to be democratic, their autocratic nature does come through. And it very quickly degenerates into a game that everyone learns to play. We learn to say what the group leader wants us to say, and we learn to play the game the way the group leader wants us to play. We learn to say what she wants to hear, or what he wants to hear, and so we're certainly becoming compliant. The Writers' Group is dramatically different from that, because it is all right to be different. It is all right to go off on your own tangent, if we don't go too dreadfully off on a tangent one way or another. There is a lot more spontaneity in a group like this. We don't have to, or want to, focus on the concerns of the people. You see we don't need a group leader to keep them focused on concerns. They don't want to talk about their concerns necessarily, but if they become comfortable enough within this setting and feel unthreatened enough within an atmosphere like this, then the feelings and the concerns will come forth on their own, and they do. Jeff isn't exactly an autocratic leader. He's probably the furthest thing from it. The way he does it is that we're here to have fun. We don't expect anything. We're not judging. We're not being measured. We're listening to each other.

We have very enjoyable times. I find, for the most part at least, that we are very mutually supportive, and I believe that we're all learning to be much less judgmental—and I think one of the real impediments to recovery from mental illness is when we begin to judge ourselves. It is a good, a very good, strong group, and I believe it is taking on a life of its own. Like I've said, it's like a home. It is a place where we can express ourselves without fear of ridicule, or embarrassment.

The writing is very, very important. In fact, it is central to the success of the group. If we were to just talk, it wouldn't be the same. The writing can be therapeutic, not in some distant and esoteric way, but in a very immediate and straightforward way.

When I first became involved with the CMHA Writers' Group I had a lot of pain to express. We either express our pain, or we can end up being victimized by it. Like many of my fellow members, there seemed to be a stage that we had to go through.

Sometimes when I wrote of these painful things, I wept. But men do not weep in public. As a precaution, at first I called upon other members of the group to read some of these sadder events in my life—the death of a child I had been very close to, the pain on the face of my small son when he was being wheeled into the operating room for surgery on a compound multiple fracture in this forearm, aspects of my mental health crisis—a broad set of the vicissitudes of life.

But something else occurred. My pain was both acknowledged and accepted by the group. This made it much easier to bear, and eventually to bury. When I had come to terms with my pain, I was able to let it rest, along with the intense anger I so frequently felt toward what so frequently seemed unjust.

Then, as I reread these accounts, I began to recall events with greater precision. They no longer loomed so large. In fact, along with the pain, I began to recall a number of very pleasant and invigorating events as well—the day I outran a big boy in a foot race, and saw the perplexity on his face when he saw me slip by him like a whisper. I remembered the delight I took when I was a baby sitter for a pair of little girls who learned to adore me and follow me around the yard with cheerful and admiring voices. I recalled amusing things, like the time when I was very small, when I kicked a football through a goal, not knowing at the time that it was my own team's goal.

With the scales of pain peeled away, I learned to laugh for the pure joy of it. The scar tissue of pain, unaddressed and left intact, can be emotionally debilitating. It can block the sunlight of a free spirit.

We are told that we cannot change the past. Objectively, this is true, but we also have a subjective self. The subjective self can learn to see with a greater, or in a more objective manner. We cannot change the past, but we can change the way we see and interpret it. This is the process of becoming whole. This has made a tremendous change to the way in which I see myself, but almost magically, it seemed to change the way I was seen by others. Children in particular were more positively responsive to me. It may be that children enjoy the company of happy people, and with my pain discarded, I was becoming a happier person.

I believe I also became a more competent writer. Subsequent to this experience I sold a few essays and short stories. But if I had not enjoyed this success, writing would still have been a very worthwhile venture.

I recommend this "therapy" very highly.

The other day, someone at Writers' Group said that writing drains his energy, and he has to be careful because it can leave him with nothing left to give. I disagree with that. It's not like that at all for me. Writing is like the magic penny—the more you give, the more you receive back.

Sometimes when I don't understand something right away, I write about it. More often than not, I start to see more clearly as I write. This is especially important at times of crisis. When I quit a university computer class last fall, I needed to understand what was going on. I wrote a short story that really helped me to understand what happened. The writing gave me a clarity that I didn't have beforehand. Writing helps me to see more clearly.

When I had to drop out of the university computer course, I had trouble accepting it. On one level, I knew I had done the right thing—the stress was simply too much and I couldn't risk falling into a crushing depression again. But on another level, I really couldn't understand it. It wasn't until I wrote a short story called "My Load Is Light" that everything made sense to me. The writing helped me discover what I was going through. I also made an attempt to understand the experience through my father's eyes—how he would see it, what he would say. I found that in writing this story, I gained a deeper understanding of who I was and what was important.

I created a character named Jason Carpenter who "loved to unravel the mysteries that shrouded the workings of complex things." After his career had ended and his children had left home, "he took a plunge, and entered university to study computer science. Initially it was exhilarating....However, just before dropping off to sleep, he would hallucinate. He saw things that indeed were not there, and he was knowledgeable enough to know they were not there....It was a crushing disappointment to Jason" who wanted to create a Web page "to reach out to others, who, like himself, had a real passion for the unusual." I ended the story with Jason having to make a choice:

> But could he meet the frustration, and the scholastic deadlines university study demanded? Would he return to the cycle of exhaustion followed by a crushing depression?
>
> A truly severe depression is a dreadful thing to experience. It is the closest experience to a descent into hell. It is small wonder to any who have made this journey to understand why one in ten of the sufferers die at their own hand.
>
> He could, on one hand, continue his studies, and access the therapeutic benefit of writing, but in a less intense way. Maybe he would hang in, and learn to laugh at his crisis. In this way, he might enjoy the best of both worlds.
>
> But he would not risk another descent. His children who now spanned three generations were too precious to take such a risk.
>
> My father used to say that discretion is the greater part of valour. He knew this as few do. With this knowledge, and the support of Francis Shaunessy, he had lived in the trenches ten months over the life expectancy of an infantry man. His career as an infantry man was undistinguished, but he lived through it. Perhaps this was the greatest victory of all.
>
> As it is, my blessings are many, and my load is light. To use the metaphor of the soldier, I believe I will apply for an extended leave.
>
> (Borley, 2000, "The Load Is Light")

Writing that story helped me to really understand my predicament, and allowed me to make an intelligent decision. I don't think I could have resolved it without writing it down, and actually looking at it. Writing gave me a little distance.

It gave me a little greater edge, a little greater objective edge. I didn't see it that clearly until I wrote it down and examined it from, through what I saw as the way my father would have seen it, and the way other people involved may have seen it. It gave a better perspective on the decision.

I find that writing is often like that. I often start to understand how I feel, or think about something, after I write about it. At Writers' Group, Jeff will sometimes give us topics that I've never thought about before. It's exciting to find out what I think, and to hear what others think about something. We grow that way.

The social aspect of the Writers' Group is very important. After we write, we always read our writing aloud. Jeff asks for volunteers and then we read in a circle. It is always important to hear what the others say. Also, you know, if someone respects your work enough to read it, then, at least, they've heard what you've had to say. They don't always agree, which is good because the way we refine our body of knowledge is by clarifying differences, and resolving conflict. Listening to others is important because we can learn how others think. It expands our horizons.

I also think reading is very important for writers. I'm an avid reader, and read between thirty and forty books a year, as well as magazines and newspapers. Reading is a window on the world. I remember my father talking about when he was overseas in England before he went over to France to fight. One afternoon he spent the afternoon having tea with an elderly lady. This would have been about 1916, and that old lady had never traveled further than 17 miles from the place she was born. And yet, she read so extensively and she got news from so many people, and wrote letters and so on. She was actually very, very aware, and very interested in world affairs, and made some very competent judgments of them. And of course she wrote as well—she wrote letters. For me, reading was my model. What I read provided most of my models. If I had a writer that I really admired, or a few writers I really admired and who seemed to really get through and present things well, I would read [their] books. Half of my attention would be on the story as it was unfolding, and the other half of my attention would be glued on how he was doing it. I didn't copy them. I used their technique. I didn't plagiarize in any sense. I think you might be able to be a good writer and not read, although where would you get the little subtleties in style? All art is deeply involved in craftsmanship, and craftsmanship has to be learned and you can learn it from examining examples of it, or practicing it, or through trial and error. But to analyze the construction of the novel or the short story, I think you would have a lot of gaps.

Jeff asked me about being heard with my writing, and the importance of my "voice" reaching people. I wrote him an e-mail about it, and it actually turned into a short essay which I called "Voices." I won't quote the whole thing. He has it somewhere and you can ask him for it if you're interested. It's interesting. Jeff keeps asking me for permission to use this or that, and my answer is always the same. It goes without saying really. Maybe by doing this study people like us can be heard and not ignored anymore. I really enjoy being part of this study. It gives me a chance to think about writing, and what it means to me.

> To be fully human, we require the opportunity to participate in the process of a shared symbolism. Language is not the single and only form of symbolism. It is, at the same time, the most versatile. It allows for the exercise of meaningful thought within a great variety of contexts. Without language, we could not have conceived of embarking on such enterprises as circumnavigating the globe, or landing a man on the moon, to name but a few. Without language, the small child could not relate to Peter Rabbit and his transgressions. With careful observation and study, we can clarify the known, but language seems to be the vehicle by which we construct hypothetical experience. So far as we know, the human is the only creature that can create hypothetical experience, and examine it critically.
>
> To be fully human, we must engage in the process of language. Language is interactive. We must speak, and we must be heard, notwithstanding the Victorian injunction that children are to be seen and not heard.
>
> We need human interaction within a number of contexts to clarify our cognition.
>
> A writing group seems to be proving itself to be one of the most effective forms of interaction. We are sharing our cognition, our shared thoughts and feelings with respect to matters mundane and profound. When we can share our symbolic world with others, expanding the boundaries of our own, and clarifying the boundaries of the thought of others, we can be led to an acceptance of the integrity of our own world, and confirm the integrity of the worlds of others.
>
> This is among the noblest of human endeavors.
>
> Let us claim this fundamental right: to have a voice, and to hear the voices of others.
>
> (Borley, 2000, "Voices")

Maybe that is why I value the Writers' Group so much. It gives each of us a place where we are accepted, and where we are heard. The writing leads to cognitive growth. And hearing other people's ideas helps out a great deal. In most social situations I tend to be a mouse in the corner. I listen a lot more than I talk. And also, the advantage to being the mouse in the corner is that I can present myself in a very non-threatening way and from this standpoint, people will convey a lot more than they would otherwise. I get an insight into how people think about things. Jeff says that is maybe why elephants are afraid of mice. I had to laugh at that. I learned to listen rather late in life. At one point I was overly candid about things like political issues and so on, and offended a lot of people and turned them off, so they turned off me, and there was no communication. So now I listen more. I don't say yes, and I don't say no.

Actually I think to be a good writer, you have to be a good listener especially if we are going to present realism. Your medium, at least if you're trying to write in a realistic way, your medium is the thoughts of people. And how do you know what people think, unless you listen? And at Writers' Group there is always a lot to listen to. If we can get a little more emotional energy packed into it, you see, that's good for learning as well as stimulating creativity.

And writing is very different than speaking. The voice box does not have a delete button. I think when we went from the oral tradition to the written tradition we expanded our horizons very, very much. The individual who told stories could only tell the stories that related to his own life experience and to maybe telling some of the stories about other people that he knew within his circle. But now when he gets access to the written word, then he can expand these horizons broadly and bring in things that he has read about—what politicians said, what ministers said, what social activists have said. You see, he has access to so much more information, and there is so much more that could be recorded. The world expands because you can refer to different books. One of the most exciting discoveries to me was to learn that I wasn't the only philosopher in the world.

Also with writing you can hear yourself. You have the opportunity to hear yourself from a new perspective after a few days or sometimes a few months. You don't get that with talking. Also, human memory, I believe, is pretty faulty. Whereas once it is on paper, it is a pretty accurate record. In fact, a lot of people are accused of lying about different things when actually they probably just learned to think differently about them than at the time they said them. They actually believe that they never said that. They've changed but they're not aware that they've changed. Whereas with your writing, then you are aware how you've revised your attitudes and opinions. Then with the Writers' Group, the big value in that is that you get feedback from within the group. I believe that when I write I usually have the chance to edit everything a couple of times to present just what I want to say. When I'm talking, I don't have that option because once I've said it, I've said it. The editing is much easier with the written word than with the spoken word because who has an accurate enough memory to recall exactly what who said, or exactly what your position is? With talking I believe very often you get stuck back in the gestalt of ideas without really fingering them, and bringing them out and giving them full form.

I especially like working with writing and ideas. I just sit down and start writing, and then when I read it over a little bit, and think, "uh, uh" I wipe that out. The writing somehow seems to take a shape and a direction on its own, and that's why I do that. I shape it like clay, somewhat similar to what a sculptor does. He has a broad gestalt of what he wants to create, and he starts shaping it, and the gestalt takes on a refinement, and he shapes it in a more refined way and a more concise way until he's got his finished work. And if it still looks like hell, he throws it into the fire. The other thing I try to do is to flow with the story. I try to avoid letting the story dictate how I deal with it, and I also try to avoid dealing with the story in a direction that it doesn't seem to want to go. A story flows. It begins and takes a flow. It takes a movement. It almost has a life of its own. But I have to balance those two elements. The trick is to balance where the story seems to want to go at the same time that I am guiding it. I'm guiding the story, and the story is guiding me. It's an interactive kind of thing. Sometimes the two processes are in conflict.

I keep a file on the computer called "Ideas." And then if I go back to it and say, "well, maybe I was kind of off the deep end at that point, or kind of out to lunch on this one, it's not going where I want it to go," I scratch it. But I usually don't keep them. Otherwise, I would have the computer full of ideas that I would never have time to develop.

One week Jeff showed us how to brainstorm, and then how to organize the ideas. It worked for some people. I think it is very good for people who find it difficult to formulate ideas, but my problem is not in formulating ideas. My problem is controlling them and keeping a lid on them. I have a bit of a problem trying to keep them down to earth.

Sometimes I write the piece, editing as I go. Sometimes I write the whole piece, and then go back and edit. I might write a paragraph, or a page or two, and it seems to be going well, and then I read it over and say, "Oh, hell, that grammar is dreadful. That sentence is really ponderous," so I rewrite it and break it up. Maybe I'd write ten pages and then go through it quickly. Sometimes something doesn't make sense and I take the whole thing out. It's a constant editing process. The main criteria I use with the story, or plot, is if it is plausible, rational, and believable. I like realism in all kinds of art. I know some people like to take paint and splash it on until it looks pretty without any relevance to the real world. Well, they have fun, but don't ask me to look at it because I don't know what they're doing. And I don't think they do either, although I would never say that.

If my grandchildren, or my great-grandchildren, or great-great-grandchildren read my writing when they're 45, I want it to be credible and believable enough so that they will have a real insight into the reality of the time in which I lived. It has to be consistent with the social reality of the time. Once I finish a piece I don't revise it then. I try to sell it. I've also made the remark, both in terms of visual art and literary art, that a good part of it is knowing when to quit.

Basically, writing enhances what I'll call the focus. It provides a very, very strong focus for my life. It makes things more vivid. When I get writing about it, I find that the act of writing tends to enhance the memory. When I start writing about something, I remember, "Oh, yes. I remember this happened that spring, too," or something of that nature. I'm not really into the imaginative. I write for realism. Even if I try to get into the imaginative, I still, as a general rule, get a focus on someone I know, and try to picture him in that imaginary setting.

My writing is usually based on things that have happened to me. I draw my characters from life. For instance, if I get this character that I am using as my focus into a situation, I try to remember what would he say, and what would he look like in this situation, and I set out to describe it. From my perspective, from trying to write with very compelling realism, all we have to relate is what we know through our experience. It is to share an experience. I like credible fiction, like John Steinbeck. He wrote in a very realistic way, and from what I have heard since, and it doesn't surprise me at all, all of his characters were drawn from real life. I really like to project realism. Fiction is the best history. Fiction does not pretend to be totally objective. Fiction allows the writer the latitude to project into what has never been objectively established, but if he is a student of human behavior, a careful student of human behavior, he can project quite well on many occasions. At the same time, in doing so, he can make the story more vivid and more compelling, he becomes a very good teacher of history. I also find it interesting to read three historical novels about the same period from three different authors, and then compare and contrast.

Writing has made me more confident now. Now that I'm aware, or more acutely aware, of my mental illness, writing is a very essential tool for coping. One of the first things that happens with a person in my situation is his mood starts going off the deep end, one way or the other. We either get depressed, or we get a little too high. I believe, I've mentioned before that it is our thinking that is at least an equal part of the mix. And the thinking and the feelings that are derived out of that thinking do change the brain chemistry. They are not separate entities. They're interrelated. I can sit down and I can start writing, and get things back into perspective and feel a little more confident about how I am going to cope with the situation. So, it has that value. I have it now. I understand what it is about now. I understand what the real issue is when you write it, and examine it. Because writing and examination go together. Writing is a self-examination process that helps you cope with things, and to examine what is important in your world.

When I started writing my novel, *Sarah Tallhorse*, I really didn't know where I was spiritually, and at the end of it, by the time I had finished it, I had concluded that the man, or the woman, or the person, who is spiritually fulfilled, had first found peace with the Great Spirit especially in how he functions across the earth and with its situations. They are at peace with the Great Spirit, and in this way, by finding peace with the Great Spirit, they can find peace within themselves. And unless they had the peace within themselves, they could not really succeed in finding peace with their fellow man. When we can find peace within ourselves, we can find peace with our fellow man and children and the animals, and all the creatures on the earth. Writing is how I defined it. You see, writing that novel is how I arrived at this perception of what spiritual peace is about. It was the self-awareness of what the spiritual is all about.

Writing is a learning process. You draw on all the things in your experience. You draw on all your observations, and you draw on all the reliable material you've been able to read. By the time you put these resources together, and put them in a situation, you can approach it with a fair level of intelligence. And to me, there is an intellectual growth, there is a spiritual growth, there is a personal growth, and, of course, you can get a lot of laughs.

When I write a story or when anyone writes a story, they are making a statement inadvertently about themselves. If the story is accepted, then again, they are accepting who you are so that strengthens your sense of identity, of who you are. I think that is a very vital component. In addition, I find that for me, writing has another very important value, especially with someone like myself who has gone through the mill with mental illness. It helps to clarify my thinking. I can write, and I can pick up what I've written and read it again in a couple of days and get a new perspective. If you can clarify your thinking, I believe, you end up having a lot more control over how you feel about things. In many cases, I think I feel much less intensely about things than I did before I got involved with this group. My fundamental identity is derived from a whole group of people that I interact with. But writing clarifies what it is for me. It adds clarity to my identity, and in this way, makes my identity much more secure. Because writing has always been such a very important part of who I am, and what I do. It identifies me in a very profound way, emotionally, intellectually and spiritually. Yes, words are the wings of thought, but oh so much more, the door to healing, the gate to magic, the key to laughter, the sense of the human spirit and soul.

Caroline Murphy

Caroline Murphy [pseudonym] is in her late forties, and has attended the Writers' Group for the last five years. She has had a very abusive past, both in her childhood and her two marriages, and the Writers' Group has been an important place of healing for her. She attended quite regularly, though she was occasionally too tired to attend after working a series of jobs she maintained to get by economically. She writes outside of the Writers' Group sessions, and has completed a full-length novel. After one of our interview sessions, I asked her if she minded if I used some of the details from our interviews to create a short story for the research project. She was very enthusiastic about that idea, and responded with happiness and surprise. "You would do that? I would really like that. I would love to see how others view me. It would really help me." I told her that I would have to get her permission in writing because I wanted to be sure of ethical considerations, and she readily agreed. What is interesting about this process is that a few weeks later she sent me a story she had written based on her experiences. As the research continued, she gave me additional writing that she felt would help me understand her life experiences, and her connections with writing. Since the writing of this book, Caroline has entered into a new relationship and has moved out of the province. She still continues to remain in contact with me and several members of the Writers' Group via e-mail correspondence.

The first-person narrative of Caroline employs fictive elements and is based on a series of in-depth interviews I conducted with her over several months. Together we decided that I would create a narrative that utilized some of the elements of a short story, allowing me to conflate the interview material with personal conversation and Caroline's writing. I was at first very hesitant to write a fictive account of her experiences, but Caroline was very adamant that she wanted her narrative to be like a short story. I feel that a fictive account of Caroline best allows me to evoke a sense of her experience at the Writers' Group, and to convey what writing means to her. The name Caroline is a pseudonym, and I have changed minor identifying details to protect her anonymity. She read early versions of this narrative account, and many of her suggestions have been incorporated in the final version.

Some of the events in the narrative are fictional. For instance, the singles dance, the scenes at her apartment, and the material dealing with her personal relationships with others, were all created by me as a way of contexualizing her experience at the Writers' Group. I wanted to show how writing and the Writers' Group permeated the whole of Caroline's life. In constructing Caroline's narrative, I did not concentrate on developing an elaborate plot, thinking that it would distract from the character and her responses to the experiences of writing and attending the Writers' Group. Diversi (1998) notes "the short story genre has the potential to render lived experience with more verisimilitude than does the traditional realist text" (p. 132). I was initially reluctant to create a fictional narrative of Caroline because I didn't want to intrude into her world, but with her encouragement and insistence, I decided to complete it. We communicated regularly, and she feels that my fictional rendering accurately tells her story, and helps her to see and interpret her own world.

One of my goals with Caroline's narrative was to create a sense of empathic understanding (Barone & Eisner, 1997), both in its creation, and in the way it is read by future readers. Nye (2000) notes that "each narrative told constructs a world of its own" (p. 391) and I wanted the reader to enter this world to gain an understanding of Caroline's experiences with writing. According to Witherell and Noddings (1991), "Stories invite us to come to know the world and our place in it" (p. 13). I have known Caroline for over five years. We maintain a close contact through the Writers' Group and her interest in understanding how she writes. I feel quite confident that the narrative represents an accurate portrayal of Caroline's experience with writing and attending the Writers' Group. Alvermann and Hruby (2003) suggest that "fictive representation attempts to use the techniques of fiction to frame and present factual data that has been gathered with all the methodological rigor appropriate to qualitative interview research, but presents this data in an aesthetically effective (and affecting) manner" (p. 261). I also had Caroline read over the narrative to confirm the voice, and the accuracy of my portrayal of her experiences. In creating the fictional narrative of Caroline, I was motivated by a quotation from Richardson (1990):

> Although life is not a narrative, people make sense of their lives and the lives of others through narrative constructions. In our work as researchers we weigh and sift experiences, make choices regarding what is significant, what is trivial, what to include, what to exclude. We do not simple chronicle "what happened next," but place the "next" in a meaningful context. By doing so, we craft narratives; we write lives. (p. 10)

Caroline made several valuable observations about my narrative, and I changed the original to reflect her perceptions. The romantic themes in the narrative echo many of the romantic themes in Caroline's writing. I have struggled with the "voice" of the story, but both Caroline and I feel that it is evocative of her perspective and I stand by it, while at the same time admitting that it is overly simplistic at times. She was very satisfied with the final result, and my creating of her narrative seemed to motivate her own writing. She also decided to write a fictional autobiography of me, which she forwarded by e-mail. Once again, the researcher and participant were involved in mutually creative acts.

The Narrative of Caroline Murphy: In the Rain

I'm sitting in my truck outside the Mental Health offices. It's raining again, and the water runs down the street in thin rivulets. The rain pounds against the cab and the old fender I have in the truck bed. The accident happened over five years ago, and I bought the fender from salvage nearly a year ago. I never seem to get anything done anymore. Sometimes I feel like the rain can wash everything away. I love the rain. I am never alone in the rain.

I feel like no one can see me. As a child I was never allowed to cry. I would stand in the rain for hours and let the raindrops run down my cheeks like tears. It was like I was letting God cry for me. I could hide in the rain. I still can't cry. I haven't cried for years and there is nowhere to hide.

I don't know why she is making me go to this mental health thing. I don't really want to attend. All those people. And what does my health have to do with anything? I know it's really about the money. It's always about money. My doctor can talk about me needing to belong, but I know it's the money. I know it is. I can feel it. Maybe she doesn't get paid if I don't join a mental health organization. Some weird government referral thing or something. I just moved here. I don't know anyone in this city. I don't want to go to this writing group thing. I don't know these people. Why should I trust them?

I've been here before, last week, to talk to the receptionist. She was actually nice. She showed me around and gave me a newsletter with all the activities listed on a calendar. I noticed the Writers' Group right away. I've always written. I've kept a journal for years, and write poetry, a lot of it around the time that Dave left. Well, that's not quite accurate. I kicked him out. No, that's not quite it either. I left him. I mean, the police did nothing. I couldn't even get a restraining order. My father protected me with a shotgun for three days. It wasn't the greatest time of my life. At least I got a lot of writing from it. When I'm outside, I'm not allowed to be real. In writing, I feel real.

I sit in the truck and watch as people go through the front door. Most of them are walking. Maybe they take the bus. One guy rides a bike. He wears an old white plastic helmet. He takes it off, and wraps it around a U-shaped bike lock and attaches the bike to the front support beam. One guy drives a grey car and carries a black canvas briefcase. He waves at me as he goes past, and he doesn't even know me. He actually noticed me. I decide that I can't stay in the truck all night. I might as well go in and get it over with. I walk into the rain, and then into the building.

———

I'm invisible. It has to be that. I've disappeared somehow. This DID thing drives me crazy. I don't even know whether to believe the doctor. Disassociative Identity Disorder. It sounds so official. I mean, doesn't everyone zone out sometimes? Maybe mother was right? Maybe I am bad, too bad to be seen anymore, or not even worth looking at.

Karen talked me into going to a singles dance last weekend. I thought it was a stupid idea, but then I actually got excited at the last minute. Everything is a contradiction. I was surprised that the red dress still fit. I'm now so fat.

We drove together, but Karen had arranged to meet someone there—a man she had met the week before. She didn't tell me until after we had paid and gone in. I was mad.

"You should have told me. This isn't fair," I said.

"You wouldn't have come if I had told you."

"Exactly. Now I'm going to sit alone all night with no one to talk to."

"Only if you want to. You're here to meet someone, aren't you? Come on, let's get a drink."

That's what she said. A drink. And Karen knows that I haven't had a drink in five years, ever since the last relationship. "Use me and abuse me." That should have been my motto. But that time I had enough. No more abuse.

"Let's get a table first," I said.

We walked across the dance floor. The church hall has a small stage at one end, and a floor marked with painted lines for basketball and volleyball. The basketball hoops were up and draped with red and green crepe paper. We sat at one of the long tables covered with white paper cut from a roll, snapped onto the corners with clothes pegs. There were a couple of plastic flowers in plastic vases at each table.

"What do you want?"

"A Coke, thanks."

"That's it? You'll be the life of the party."

"You know I don't drink."

"Never?" And she walked away to get the drinks.

———

Whenever I spoke out, Dave would reach over and hit me. Once when I called a friend, he grabbed the telephone and slashed the receiver against my forehead. My friends stopped calling. I went deeper and deeper into myself until I couldn't find me anymore. It was a place I was getting to know very well. I started to feel that I had nothing to say. I had no voice, no words.

People ask me why I stayed with him for so many years. Seven and a half years. That's really not that long. Why didn't I leave? That's hard to answer really. The kids—Megan and Rachel—were everything to me. I would sacrifice myself for them. I would do anything for them. I had no money of my own, no job. I had nothing to offer them. I had no choice. But when he hit my son, that's why I left.

Karen's friend shows up. He buys us each another drink and then they go dance together. I sit at the empty table leaning against the wall. It is just like high school. What was it they called us? The wallflowers. No one ever saw us there either. I'm not here. I'm not here. I'm not here.

The Writers' Group meets in a large room behind the receptionist's desk. Inside the room, the tables are pushed together, and it's like they form a square circle. I mean, the tables are square, but the people around the tables are in a circle—the circle and the square. It's like we're all joined together somehow. It's stupid. I wonder whose idea that was? I don't want to connect with these people.

I want to sit at the back of the room, but there is no back. There is really no place to hide. People are talking and laughing. Everyone is crazy here. What am I doing here? Someone has made coffee. The man next to me asks if I want any. He says there are cups in the kitchen. I brought a small notebook, but I can't find a pen in my purse. Someone across the table slides me a pen.

The room has three arches and the ceiling is covered with what looks like white insulation. The arches are separated by two wooden beams, each with a four-bladed fan attached to it. The windows have Venetian blinds on the lower parts, and are covered with white paper at the top. A green door leads to the kitchen. A book case is on the far wall with an upright piano in front of it. On the piano is a small sign that reads: "Remember. No Dancing on the Piano." There is another poster that reads: "Ends: What Benefits? Delivered to What People? At What Cost?" I never used to notice anything. I can see stuff since Dave left.

Chairs are scattered around the room. At least one of them is broken. A counter runs along one wall with a water cooler on top. Behind me are a green chalkboard and a cork bulletin board made of a series of smaller tiles. A flip chart and some paper rest on a table by the wall. The carpet is green—someone called it sea-foam green. Maybe the tables are like lifeboats on a sea of green. I like the green, but I wish there were some plants.

The guy with the briefcase is named Shawn. He is obviously the leader of the group. The receptionist told me about him. She said that he's been doing volunteer work here for about eight years. He seems to laugh a lot. He makes a point of having everyone in the group introduce themselves and say a little bit about what they've been doing all week. When he gets to me I am very nervous and I don't know what to say. He doesn't seem to mind. He asks me if I have paper and a pen, and then he says that he only has one rule. Oh right, here goes another male with a need to control. Instead he simply says that I have to have fun. Have fun? What kind of rule is that? Is he serious? No one ever lets me have me have fun anymore. Okay, I'll listen. For awhile.

———

I remember once in school I wrote a poem. It must have been about grade nine. I was so proud, so happy that I accomplished a poem. I never thought I would be able to do that. I gave it to my teacher. I probably had a huge grin on my face. My teacher was a man, and he took the poem from me and read it at his desk. Then he looked up at me. I was still grinning.

"You think this is funny?"

"What?"

"This poem. You think this is funny?"

"No."

"Whose is this, Caroline? It's simply too good to be yours. You didn't write this. Did you copy it from a book? Do you think I'm stupid or something? Is that why you're smiling? Go back to your desk and write something else, something that I know is yours."

The poem was called the "Land of Love." And I made copies of it, but they all disappeared. I hid them in different places and they all disappeared. I remember very little of it. I didn't write another poem for years. Why bother? Nobody ever believed you. Why risk the pain?

———

I shake my head. A woman beside me has her hand on my shoulder. She smiles. Shawn asks if I'm okay. I must have disappeared. I'm embarrassed, but no one seems to mind. No one says anything about me being strange. They just leave me alone. One guy asks if we can start writing. He seems anxious to begin.

Everyone at Writers' Group has their own book and pens, and seems to know what they are doing. They are all anxious to get started writing. In the middle of the tables are a couple of dictionaries and a thesaurus. Shawn is busy talking to the woman next to him. She hands him a piece of paper and waits while he reads it. He looks up and nods. She smiles. He leans back to the paper and makes a couple of marks on it. She nods her head and smiles again. She sits down and Shawn introduces a topic we can write on, though he says we can always write about anything we want. I think he said to write about "justice." What is amazing is that as soon as he finishes talking everyone starts writing. It seems like a race or something, with everyone trying to get all their ideas down at once. Even Shawn writes.

―――

I love my apartment. I just painted it all white. Someone said it would open up everything. It's so clean now, and I love the light. I have plants everywhere. I love plants. I have ten of them in my apartment. They don't talk back, and they don't lie to me. And most of all, they are alive. I used to kill plants and my daughter wouldn't let me have any. Then in my second marriage, I put plants in the front room and my husband wouldn't come in there. He wouldn't go in the light and happy room. The plants were life to me. When I moved back to the prairies I brought my plants with me. I have a white couch and a big chair that I sit in and listen to music. Sometimes I light candles. I like the way the shadows move in the room.

Sometimes I like writing in my apartment. I usually write at my kitchen table, but sometimes I like writing in bed. I sit up and rest the pad of paper on my knee and can just write and write. It's like the real me can come out then.

It's hard to know what to write sometimes. I write in what I suppose could be called a journal. It scares me sometimes. I mean, what if someone finds it and reads it? What would they think? Whose book is it then? Would they think that I'm dirty? That's what my mother used to say about me all the time. I never let my family read my writing. Writing is too risky.

―――

At the Writers' Group we write for about ten or fifteen minutes at a time. It's amazing really. I haven't written anything for over a year, and here I have a page and a half in no time. Shawn asks for volunteers to read aloud. I didn't know about this. I can't read my stuff aloud to everyone else. They'll know what an idiot I am. I don't have anything to say. My writing sucks right now.

We go around in a circle. Everyone reads though Shawn said before we started that anyone could pass if he or she wanted. No one passes. Everyone is so good. I can't believe it. When he gets to me, he asks me if I want to read. Then he says that I don't have to. I don't know what happened, but there I am reading my stuff. After I finished, someone said I should read at a coffee house or something. That my writing was good. They really liked it. I start crying, and the weird thing is no one says anything. They just let me cry and keep talking about what I had written. Pretty soon I'm laughing. They just accept me for who I am. I can't remember the last time that happened. I am calm for the first time in years. No doctor could do that for me. No medication could do that for me. It is the writing, and this room, and these people.

———

I wrote a novel before I joined the Writers' Group. I was driving to the coast with my parents to visit my kids, and the book just hit me. It wrote itself. I couldn't stop writing that book. It's a long, romantic kind of thing. I know that, but I can't cut any of it. It is too close to me. When I wrote it I was just writing, the writer just wrote. And when she was finished, the person who dealt with the next phase appeared.

Writing helped clarify my life. Maybe it didn't clarify my life, but it helped. I just dumped my life by taking it from inside, and putting it outside in such a way that I could I read it, and other people could too. Maybe it is important to communicate to other people because maybe it can help. Abuse is awful. I mean, it didn't help me that much then, but maybe it can help somebody else deal with their problems sooner than I did. Writing about being in that life helped. It kept me from being totally alone, I guess. I had the characters in the book. The writing wasn't draining, but there was an emptiness when it was done. It was a gift. When I write, things start to make sense for me. And if I can have someone read what I write, then I can get them to listen or hear me. I know that sounds strange, but when I talk, people don't listen to me. It's when I write that they listen.

———

Shawn is kind of a quiet guy. He keeps a lot of himself inside and is very careful of what he says. He usually sits at the far end of the tables, and spreads out his papers in front of him. I tease him about hiding behind his books. I can do that now. He lets us talk before we write, and then again after each of us has read. He's got a hard job actually. He has to keep things rolling along, but he can't be obvious about it. After all it's not school, and we wouldn't be here if it was just like school. Maybe that is why he seems to hide. Maybe he doesn't want to get in the way. I don't know.

I wish he would read his stuff more. He is so busy now that he rarely reads his short stories or essays. His father died a couple of years ago, and his mother now has cancer. Reading that stuff aloud would probably do him good. Maybe if he realized that releasing himself in the writing would help us even more, he would read more often.

Why I write is a very, very interesting question. When I write I release feelings, frustrations. It's artistic. It's everything. I can take what is inside and release it outside. I get to release hate there as well. I don't allow myself to release hate in my life. I don't allow it to surface. In writing it is released and that is good because then it is outside of me. If you keep it in, it becomes you. When you keep everything in control and in perspective, you become the controls instead of who you really are. You lose everything. I look at some people and they have lost so much of who they are. They don't even know who they are anymore. They don't know what is good for them. They don't know what they want. They think that they know what they want because the conscious mind says that this is what they're supposed to want. But it's not. They've lost who they are.

When you write, everything is thrown outside of yourself. It is taken outside of your being, and that is really important so it doesn't become you. If pain is kept inside and never expressed, or never talked about, or never realized, it becomes you. And people will say to themselves that they have forgotten the pain, or have managed to put it somewhere. A lot of people don't remember it. But the mind never forgets it, so it comes out in other ways. If you don't express anger, anger will come out towards someone else or something else. Because if you are feeling angry, and you don't have any place to put it, you will put it on somebody else. Believe me. I know. Writing releases these feelings and then they don't become part of you. Before Writers' Group, I was never allowed to have an imagination.

I even make changes now. I didn't used to. I usually make them at the end, when I'm finished. I learned I had to make some changes. The mind works faster than your pen or typing even though I'm a pretty fast typer. I just fix some sentence structure and grammar. I don't do any spelling. I let the computer do that. Sometimes I over express myself, or over explain. I like to cut the babble. My novel is different though. I had to write it by hand, and then type it later. I made some corrections in my head when I was typing so that my feelings were more clearly expressed.

It's interesting. I didn't consciously relate events in my life to events in the novel. I was still splitting into different personalities when I wrote the novel. When I was finished, it was one of the personalities that came out. My editor came out. That is one of the adults inside. She is logical and will look at sentence structure and punctuation and whether I have said anything. She can be very critical, but kind too. When I'm writing I don't want to hear those voices. Because you see I'm not just one person and I never want to be. I want to be all the parts of me, because that is what makes a rounded human being. A truly rounded human being is a person who is many different facets. In this room I'll be one person, when I go out there, I'll be another. But I don't want to be a phony out there. I want to be just a part of myself. I am a survivor. I don't really see myself as a victim anymore. Writing helped me to understand that.

―――

It seems like the last year has just flown by. The Writers' Group is the one place I can be myself. It doesn't matter if I'm down or not. I'm accepted for who I am, and that brings out my creativity. I love the interactions with the other people. That is so important. People are accepted here. We get into some amazing debates. We talk about politics, and abuse, and women's rights, and the police, and our lives and families. It's like we can talk or write about anything. Shawn usually has a list of ideas we can write about, but if something comes up he lets us write about that. One day, he asked a man who was new at the group if he had any topics, and the man answered, "no." But instead of getting mad, Shawn says to him, "Good topic. Let's write about saying no, or ever having said no, in your life, or wishing that you had said no." Shawn is like that. He just makes stuff up and the writing that happens is amazing. You should have seen what people wrote about—regrets, happiness, coincidences, travel. All from that silly idea of saying no. And the new guy starts laughing with the rest of us.

―――

I don't have any time for myself. I work at two jobs—looking after kids all day, and cleaning apartments at night. I don't have any time for anything. No one really cares about me. I can't find the energy to attend Writers' Group. It is too much. Everything is too much.

I don't see Karen anymore. She isn't real. She isn't a real friend. She asks me to talk about my life, but she only wants me to talk about the good things. I tell her my life then is only about two paragraphs long. She says I should make up a life.

I now babysit two little girls, Erin and Jody, all day. I met their Mom at the grocery store and we got talking. I used to do this work on the coast. I also looked after elderly people at a retirement home. I like this kind of work, but sometimes there is no rest. You don't ever get to take a break.

I never seem to have any time to myself. All day the kids are running around. I don't have a minute to myself. I want to get back to writing something, anything, but I can't think. My life seems so dark.

When Erin and Jody finally leave, I have nothing left. They're not bad kids. They just have too much energy. I've already been through this. My daughters already have kids. I'm a grandmother three times over. I should be babysitting them. But they are so far away. What went wrong? I never seem to get anywhere.

I watch the rain. It looks so peaceful and so beautiful. I wish I could run into it and disappear.

People with DID are invisible. Others don't even know what the initials mean. Disassociative Identity Disorder. Is that so hard to remember? No. I got mad at Writers' Group tonight. I don't know why. No one recognizes DID. Even though I'm not splitting anymore, no one sees me. Schizophrenics are seen. They are recognized. They even have their own organization. People with DID are invisible. No one cares. No one sees them. It makes me so angry.

Maybe I'm mad because I gave Shawn my novel. I'm really excited but scared. I've never let anyone read it before. I didn't tell him that. I should never have given it to him. Never. Never. He won't read my novel. Why should he? I'm invisible.

It's strange. I don't think anyone really sees me. I mean, no one will even dance with me. Sometimes it seems like it is only at Writers' Group that I feel real.

But can I trust these people? Can I trust Shawn?

It's raining again. I sit on the couch in my apartment and watch through my front window. The trees are bending over from the pressure of the rain. Erin and Jody are playing on the floor. They seem to know not to be so loud today. I don't feel like doing anything today. I don't feel anything. Maybe I should run into the rain. Maybe I would melt away.

I'm mad. That's all I can say. I should have known better. Shawn is just like all men. They never, never do what they say. I never should have trusted him. He's had my novel for six months. I know that when I gave it to him he said that he was really, really busy. He says he is busy writing and teaching, but screw that. He could have read it by now. I don't know why I thought he was different. He just lies like them all. Doesn't he know how important this is to me?

I just wanted him to read the novel. I didn't want him to correct it or anything. I know it was five hundred pages, but he reads all the time. If he didn't have time, he should just have told me instead of lying to me. I sent him a letter telling him why I haven't been to Writers' Group and why I'm so mad. He'll probably just ignore me.

I miss the Writers' Group. I wonder what they are writing about tonight?

Shawn calls me and asks how everything is going. He tells me that he's finished reading the novel, and asks me if I want to talk about it. Of course I want to talk about it! He just laughs. He asks when I'm coming back to Writers' Group. I say I might make it next week. He says that would be great. Everyone has missed me. Is that true?

I've made such a fool of myself. Shawn must hate me. But what is weird is that he is still talking to me as if I'm real. He even invited me to some literary award that he won. His mom was there, and his girlfriend was there and they both talked to me as if I were a person. He invited three of us from the Writers' Group. Albert and Brian both wore suits. They looked very distinguished. I even wore a dress that used to fit. I must be losing weight.

When Shawn received the award and went on stage he read something that each of us from the Writers' Group had written. He thanked all of us. It was strange to hear my name over the microphone.

I think I met someone last night. Karen called after I hadn't seen her or heard from her for months. We went to another singles dance. I wore the same dress that I had worn to Shawn's award night, the one that both he and his girlfriend had said I looked so good in. This time I tried sitting not so much at the back this time and someone actually asked me to dance.

His name is Alex, and he said that I looked beautiful. No one has said that to me for years. In fact, I can't remember the last time that anyone said that to me. We danced most of the night, even the slow ones. I barely talked to Karen all night. I think I'm going to see him again.

I have the day off. I love sitting in the silence of the apartment when no one is around. Alex said he might call later and I'm looking forward to seeing him. Right now I'm happy in my own thoughts. I've been writing a lot of poems lately. I wrote one about coming out of the darkness and being in the light. I really like that one.

Writing is a part of me. It is a big part of who I am. It isn't totally who I am, but I know that there is part of me that is very much a writer, and a good writer.

Writing is like a puzzle. You throw it up in the air and then you write it, it all comes down and connects.

I hope it rains today. I want to walk in the rain. I would love to walk with Alex in the rain. I would love to share that with him. There's so much I want.

Albert Chatsis

Albert Chatsis is a sixty-eight-year-old man who has been coming to Writers' Group since it began over ten years ago. "I was the very first member," he claims, "back when it was run briefly by a man who also did vocational education, before the nurses tried to run it. It only worked when you and Sam just let us write." Albert writes everything in longhand on loose-leaf paper. He used to give his writing to Sam or me to be typed. Now he gives it to his friend Warren, who types it up on the computer and e-mails it to me each week. He used to have a writing notebook, but now often works on single sheets because he doesn't want to lose the entire book and all his writing. Albert writes slowly and carefully during the writing sessions. He also works at home, writing a long narrative about Horsechild, his adopted grandfather, who was the son of the famous Canadian Cree leader, Big Bear.

Albert Chatsis' narrative was problematic in many ways, and in the end I structured it somewhat differently from Brian's narrative. At first, I wrote a narrative that was quite similar to Brian's in terms of structure; however, while I feel very confident that I "captured" the essence and voice of Brian, I was not as sure I was as successful with Albert. Albert is a Cree man, born on Poundmaker Reserve, but who has lived most of his life off the reserve. Albert speaks English with long pauses and is somehow able to use silence to create meaning. (This idea isn't as naïve as one might first suppose. For instance, Miles Davis, often working with Gil Evans, utilized the concept of silence as an object in several albums, including *Sketches of Spain, In a Silent Way* and *Kind of Blue*. Davis once said, "I always listen for what I can leave out" [cited in Sluyter, 2001, p. 79].) Albert's unique presence was extremely difficult to evoke in his narrative using a straight first-person account. While the words I used were accurate in the translations from oral interview to tape recording to transcript to narrative, something vital was missing.

I decided to alternate the first-person narrative with brief vignettes to show slightly different perspectives of Albert's experiences at the CMHA Writers' Group. In some ways I modeled the structure on Hemingway's first collection of stories, *In Our Time*, in which he alternated short stories with short poetic vignettes. Though the subject matter was usually very different in Hemingway's work, the two types of writing in juxtaposition somehow seem to illuminate specific themes and ideas. In using a combination of first-person narrative and vignettes I was hoping to capture some of the humor and personal detail that was missing in a strictly first-person narrative.

The resulting narrative is based on a series of in-depth interviews I conducted with Albert over several months. I also utilized my journal entries, as well as my personal correspondence with Albert over the last ten years. My intent with this narratives is to evoke and recreate Albert's experience at the Writers' Group, and to show the value that writing has in his life. Albert freely gave his consent, and checked over my narrative several times to ensure accuracy and to offer comments and suggestions, most of which were incorporated in further revisions. I created the vignettes, which will appear in italics, from my observations and entries in the reflexive journal I kept during the study. At times I re-created dialogue, but always with the intent of showing the experience as clearly as possible.

I gave Albert a copy of the narrative. After he finished reading it, he looked up with a smile. "It's funny," he said, "but not all the time. I like it. You captured my feelings. I really like it."

The Narrative of Albert Chatsis: Exposing the Past

I've been coming to the Writers' Group for about ten years. I was the first member. Before Sam and Jeff took over the group, it had failed many times over the years because people have done it the wrong way. Like, when David [pseudonym] was there he wanted everybody to start publishing right away. He went and got about 160 magazine addresses, and put them out on the table, and said to send your writing here, and send your writing all over the place. He thought we could make money with the writing. It just didn't work. He taught work education at CMHA. Then a couple of nurses ran it, but it didn't work again.

Now the Writers' Group works. Jeff gives us different topics each week to write about. We read them and talk about things. At first it was therapeutic to release inside pressure. If I wrote them out and exposed them to others I could let go. I couldn't let go in the past, like childhood problems, because of my nervous breakdown twelve years ago when I was hospitalized.

Writers' Group has helped me a lot. It has changed me in my mind. I am a different person altogether because of it. I think differently now. I think different. I think I am a kinder person. I'm an easier person to get along with, but I haven't written all the changes that have taken place in my brain, in my head. I'm not an angry person. I'm a creative person now.

It is important to share ideas at the writing group. The writers' group has changed me because I have talked about different things that were sympathetic. You get comments from people who feel that you've said something, and it's not only me, there are a lot of people. The social feeling at the writing group is important. You belong. Like, I go to church. I go to different churches. I don't just eat there, but I go there too, to socialize. And this is the same thing. The Writers' Group is a place where I can go and it is not going to cost me nothing. I could go to the bowling club. I can go to the hockey game. I can go to the baseball game, but I'm not interested in them. At the Writers' Group we have to work, but that is fun because it makes my brain work. That is good because if you don't make your brain work it is going to die off. Like anything else, if you don't use it you lose it. So, I use my brain to try and think up some ideas, something to come up with. If it could improve things better I would bring it up.

The books we put out every year are very, very important to me. When you write something it is different than when you speak. I can read it to myself. It's emotional. When you tell a story, the listener tells the story to the next person a little different and then the next person with a little more twist, and pretty soon I'm a different person in the story. They might make me a little bit better, or a little bit worse. The teller wants to impress. It all gets twisted around, exaggerated, or impressed in some way. But if I write it down it becomes true as I know it at that moment.

Everyone is a storyteller. If I died tomorrow, the story would still be here, would still exist. If someone tells a story it sometimes gets fantastic or unusual.

Stories get built according to who tells the story. Stories are manufactured to please the person telling it. Details can be changed. It doesn't mean nothing. In the story about my son, I could change the boy to a girl, or maybe the women cured him in the end. The mother, she could recover or die. But you will be a different person. If it gets written down, the story can't get twisted around. It is a healing thing to do that because I accomplished something, things that are important. It is a lot worse if you have a mental illness to remember things correctly. When you write or paint you let out your inner deep thoughts. When you talk you don't tell the whole truth. The trick is that when you are speaking you're thinking about what the other person is thinking. It changes what you say.

Warren and Albert

Albert and his friend Warren usually arrive fifteen minutes late. Warren always enters first, apologizing and asking what the topic is. He sometimes sits at a table leaning against the wall. Albert shuffles in after Warren, hiding in the wake. He never says a word and always smiles at me as he gets a chair and squeezes in. He gets out his paper and pen, and leans over to the person sitting next to him and asks what we are writing about. He manages to slip in quietly now that he has had both knees replaced. Before the operations he would lurch in, breathing heavily.

Warren and Albert are very good friends and have an almost symbiotic relationship. Albert gives Warren rides to the Writers' Group, and Warren types out all of Albert's writing. Warren lived in virtual isolation for over nine years after being released from the North Battleford psychiatric centre. The Writers' Group seemed to act as a catalyst, getting Warren involved in a larger social world. Albert picks Warren up at his apartment and they go to the Salvation Army and several churches both for the services and the free meals. They seem to have a detailed schedule all worked out. In December they manage four or five Christmas dinners every year.

Albert is difficult to tie down to a specific time to do the interviews. After one of the Writers' Group meetings in December, I suggest to Albert that we stay for an interview. Warren is waiting for a ride home, but he agrees to wait downstairs and watch television. Albert and I sit at one of the folding tables we use for Writers' Group, the tape recorder between us, and talk for over an hour. Warren comes upstairs after the interview. He looks like an absent-minded teacher covered in chalk. He had made coffee, spilled the coffee whitener on himself, and then fallen asleep on the couch.

After the interview I take Albert and Warren to KFC for the Toonie Tuesday special. It is about thirty-five below zero. My car barely moves. I meet them there. Eating with them is an adventure. They insist on separate gravy containers. They buy the small drinks because refills are free and the small drinks are cheaper. I say this is my Christmas present to them. It is interesting talking with them at the restaurant because they act and interact completely differently in public spaces. The CMHA writing group provides them with a stable social situation—they are safe around the table with the structure of the group. There is also probably a stabilizing factor with me running the group. Even when I'm not there, the organizational structure remains to provide stability and form. In the KFC eating area, they focus on the food. Albert spills gravy on his sweater. When I point it out he lifts his sweater and licks it off. Warren leans his forearm in the gravy he's spilled on the table. A woman and her daughter from the Crocus drop-in centre sit at a booth near our table. They shyly say hi. Albert says, "We're the Writers' Group from CMHA" with obvious pride. "This is Jeff. He's our leader of the writing group." Then Albert and Warren resume eating.

"Thanks, Jeff. This is a really good Christmas dinner."

And it is.

I write for me, to release my inner things. I write for other people because it is unusual. You find truth. When you write, it is to be seen and heard. When you speak you are only speaking about thoughts at that time. When you write, you are able to write with emotion about events now, and things in the past. The thing you write about is the shock—the changes within you. When I wrote the story "Coyotes" it gave me a sense of being there, of being with my grandfather and my grandmother and being with the coyotes again. When you write you can explain it a lot better. If you try to talk about it later your mind changes, or it is congested and your feelings have changed. If I was to retell the story it wouldn't be the same. When you write, it is not as you speak it, but as you see it inside your mind, but also with your feelings inside. It is rewarding and satisfying for me because it means something that no human has done before. With speaking it stops right there, and it's only one person. Everything ends there.

Luck

I'm in a foul mood. For the last few years, I've been balancing volunteering at the Writers' Group and teaching university English classes as an itinerant sessional lecturer. I've just arrived at Writers' Group after teaching a first-year university English class in a small city approximately a hundred miles northwest of where I live. I had left early in the *morning but still ran late. In a vain attempt to get there on time, I tried to make up time. Instead of making the class on time, I got pulled over by the RCMP [Royal Canadian Mounted Police] and presented with a speeding ticket.*

I spent the day teaching Othello, and then home (this time within the speed limit) barely making it in time to get something to eat and then hurry to Writers' Group. During the introduction to the writing session, I tell the story of my experience of getting a speeding ticket. At the end of the story, almost everyone is considerate, and expresses concern. That is, everyone except Albert Chatsis.

"You're lucky," says Albert.

"Lucky? How do you figure that? I have to pay a ticket for $110 and I can't afford it right now."

"You're still lucky," says Albert. "At least you have a car that can go that fast."

And he laughs.

When I write, I don't make notes. I've got 10,000 stories in my head. And they are true stories. I've always been interested in people's lives. I don't make an outline. I just follow the story. With the Horsechild story, I just follow what Horsechild said. I don't correct it or make changes. I write the story in order of what happened. I don't change it because I'm not making up the story. I'm telling the story the way it was told to me. If it is wrong, if it doesn't make sense, I'll leave it. I'm repeating the story as it was told to me. My grandfather would never mislead me. I trusted him one hundred percent. I'm writing a true story. There is no fiction on it. There is nothing that I've read from anyplace else, from anybody else. I've read a lot about Big Bear and Horsechild and everybody else, but I just erased that from my head. Because I didn't think it was true, and because I don't believe it.

I don't worry about spelling, sentences, or punctuation. I don't worry because you try to tell your story the best way that you possibly can. The editor who is going to do the editing for you will see to it that it is placed well. I believe in that. I take a chance. It's not the job of the writer to do that. The job of the writer is to tell the story the best way he can. As a writer, I'm telling the story the best way I can because that is how I heard it. I'll make changes at the end because the story has overlapped somehow, or I didn't tell it the right way. Like the Horsechild story right now, where I am right now, there are about three different corrections I have to make on it. I'll make those at the end.

I like writing about different topics. I have a lot of things on my mind all the time. There is this religion. There is this way of life in Canada. There is this communism. There's all kinds of things. There's politics, there's Indian beliefs,

Native Spirituality. There is my artwork. There is my writing. There's my Toastmasters. And then besides that, I love writing about Horsechild, my grandfather. I worship my grandfather because I think he was an honest man, and I believe he is an honest man. And I believe that my grandmother was an honest woman, a very honest woman. There are so many things. My life experience.

But I can't seem to finish my writing right now. There is too much interference. But I do have a lot of stories. I have not been writing because I have been having an awful lot of trouble and it interferes with my life. With all this stuff going on in it. I put my full time into it. I have been having problems. A lot of woman troubles lately, that I can't write. You see, when I'm with a woman I have less problems. I can't write when I'm emotionally upset. I want to finish the Horsechild story, but there is always pressure, pressure, pressure. And now there is pressure about this legal summons. These distractions just keep building more and more and more and more. I have to figure out a way to put a lot of these things to the side, and concentrate on finishing this story on Horsechild.

I just got to force myself to do it because it is very important to me. It is easier to get distracted. Like this court order. But you know the large number they want me to pay? About ten years ago this would have kind of scared me with this bottom number here. But because of the Writers' Group, this doesn't frighten me anymore. I know I can fight it, and win it. I've learned a lot from the Writers' Group. Me and Warren have fought with the police for the last three years. We wrote letters back and forth. When I saw them load up Lawrence Wegner, and after his body was found I knew I had to say something. The police have been doing this for years. Maybe at one point in my life, I would have been too scared to report it. Because I didn't want to get involved. At the Writers' Group we talk and write. I can even bring it up at the Writers' Group, and we can talk about it. The Writers' Group gives me courage.

Coffee

"Do you mind if I take the rest of this coffee?"

Albert is already filing his thermos bottle with the coffee left over from the writing session.

"Sure. No problem."

"Thanks. I can drink this tomorrow morning."

"Albert, can I ask you a question?"

"Yeah," he says as he pours coffee whitener into the neck of the thermos.

"Do you think it is a good idea to write about controversial topics?"

"Very important."

"Why?" I ask.

"Because you get to hear what other people think, what they believe. You can just listen. You don't have to change your mind. I don't always agree with everything. But it is interesting."

"Is that why it is good to read aloud?"

"It is good. You get to hear other ideas. It expands your brain. You learn about things. Your world grows. Are you sure you don't want any of this coffee? It's good."

Writing is a way of exposing the past, all my successes, things that I have done that were quite successful. Otherwise they are lost forever, what I did, what I accomplished. Like when I was selling guns for multi-millionaires. I know all my guns inside out, from the 1700's, the first cannons that were made, the wheel locks, the flintlocks, the matchlocks, percussion caps. I know all the guns and all the gun manufacturers. I like to write about old native ways and spirituality. I think it is important to expose the things that have happened to the people. There is no justice.

I like to write and paint about things that are unusual. It satisfies me. I like writing about my life—my own life is important. I think I've accomplished a lot in my life. It is important to expose, because you get to know the difference between a very sad situation and a very happy situation. I've always been interested in people's lives. I want my grandchildren and my great-grandchildren to know. Mostly I couldn't care less if anybody else wants to read what I write, but I know my great-grandchildren, and my grandchildren are going to be curious someday. When you write, you have to be honest with everyone someday. Writing is another way for people to learn what happened.

The Art Show

I'm standing in front of one of Albert's paintings at an art show that was a combination of writing and art displays. Albert had painted a cartoon caricature of the city police beating a native man in a deserted area. The painting was done after it became public knowledge that the city police had been accused of driving native men out of town and making them walk home to sober up. The problem with this scenario was that this was done in the dead of winter with temperatures of forty below. At least two native men had been found frozen to death.

Another painting showed Horsechild being sent home in the middle of winter after the trial of his father Big Bear. Albert had again painted a series of cartoon caricatures of police, military, government and religious leaders gathered around the figure of Horsechild.

Albert comes up beside me sipping a cup of coffee in a Styrofoam cup.

"She wouldn't let all my writing be in the show," said Albert.

"Who wouldn't?"

"Bonnie. The art instructor. She said they would get us in trouble."

"Maybe she didn't get it ready in time. She didn't exactly give us a lot of time to get things typed and framed."

"No, it was ready. I think it was because I was critical of the Catholic Church."

"Are you sure, Albert? Maybe she's just disorganized. I mean, she didn't even tell me about the show until last week. It didn't give me a lot of time to organize the writing. Maybe she just had too much to do before the show."

"No. She got the writing. She's worried that the Church will get angry and this is their gallery. She didn't want any trouble. Isn't that censorship?"

"Maybe. Do you want me to talk to her?"

"No. Don't bother. Can they go in the book?"

"Of course they can go in the book. Did you think I wouldn't let them go in?"

"I thought they might try and stop you."

"Don't worry, Albert. They will all be in the book."

The Horsechild story is the most important thing to me in my life. Horsechild was my father—he was my grandfather, but he legally adopted me, and my sister. Horsechild was the most courageous human being on earth to walk home at only twelve years old, 600 miles. Nobody else could do that. He didn't walk as the crow flies. He walked the best way that he could, trying to find the best places where he could stay and camp for awhile where there was lots of dry wood and lots of things like that. In the middle of the winter. He left Regina after the trial of Big Bear, and walked home to his reserve. He left in early mid-November and he arrived home at the end of March.

It is very important to put these things down. It should be exposed—the way this country was built. By writing I can leave something. It is important to me. I have been writing the book for several years. I want to publish it so others can learn the true story. People need to know what has happened. Through my writing they could know that. The other books on Big Bear and Horsechild are full of lies [Albert is referring here to Bleasdell Cameron's (1950/1926) *Blood Red the Sun* (original title: *The War Trial of Big Bear*) and J. R. Miller's (1996) *Big Bear (Mistahimusqua)*].

Cameron died in 1951. He wrote *The War Trial of Big Bear* and he lied all the way through. He came and visited Horsechild in 1948. I heard him talk. He must have been feeling kind a sicky, or not feeling well, or uncomfortable. Cameron and Horsechild were friends when they were small, but yet he wrote a terrible story about Big Bear, *The War Trial of Big Bear*. Big Bear never fought against anybody, but he wrote that, and he made himself such a hero. And I did hear him come and tell Horsechild in 1948. He came to my reserve, and I happened to be there. I was 14 years old. So, I could speak English enough, and understand English enough. But Cameron spoke Cree, good Cree. I was listening to him, and he said how sorry he was that he wrote that book, and that he was going to change it. Change the whole thing. But he never did. He just put out the same book and this time called it *Blood Red the Sun*. It is the same book. He just changed the title. But he did say that, and he didn't tell the truth about going to change the whole book. He told Horsechild that he had lied because he wanted to make himself, like, brave. Like a brave person. Yet Horsechild's mother saved his life. Horsechild saved his life first by going and getting him. It was already getting a bit dark, but Horsechild had this buffalo robe and covered him with it. And he walked with him, and took him down to their tent. Horsechild saved him by wrapping him in a buffalo robe and then taking him to his mother's, and his mother looked after him. His mother put on a bunch of blankets, and Cameron went under Horsechild's mother's dress, and covered him underneath there.

This happened at Frog Lake. People call it a massacre but that was not a massacre. That was a shoot out. A massacre is when you go and kill people and they are unarmed. That is a massacre. But they were both armed—these ones with arrows, and these other ones with guns. But they overtook them, they overtook the white man, took their guns and shot with them instead of the arrows.

The main killer at Frog Lake was really a brave person, and his name was Wandering Spirit. Wandering Spirit killed Quinn. It was either him or this other guy, Quinn, the Indian agent. Thomas Quinn. So Thomas Quinn grabbed his rifle which was hanging on the wall. He grabbed it, and he said I can kill you and nothing will happen to me. That's what he said to Wandering Spirit. But Wandering Spirit grabbed the gun from him before he could load it, even though he was a tall, strong man, Quinn. He was with the Seventh Cavalry. He was an American, half Sioux, and spoke Sioux. Indian Affairs hired him. Indian Affairs hired a lot of military people from the States at that time. He was one of them, and killers, like that. And he was a real killer, a bad person. Quinn killed other people in the United States, before he came to Frog Lake.

When Quinn grabbed his gun, Wandering Spirit jumped on the counter and grabbed the gun from him, and loaded it himself, and shot him. But he didn't shoot him right there. Quinn took off. He couldn't hang on to the gun, even though he had it in his hand, but this Wandering Spirit was also a very strong person, just a powerful person. And he just took the gun away from him, and as he was running away, he shot him, and killed him. Then he decided that he was going to kill everybody. Because everybody was hungry—children were hungry, and they had all kinds of food there in the warehouse. So he killed people there to feed hungry children and mothers. So he killed for a good reason, and that is why I would like to get his body or a monument set up for him on Poundmaker Reserve because Wandering Spirit was a hero to me.

KI-WE-TIN-NOW (Winter's Home)

Big Bear pointed his pipe to all four Directions, to all the mighty forces of Nature. Also to his spiritual guides, the great father, and the great Bear and to the earth. You are so kind to us with abundant supply of food. We are grateful.

These words of prayer were very touching and seeing into his poor brain, a real suffering brain, because his father sounded so serious. Then Big Bear sang songs, spiritual songs.

Big Bear turned to his guarding spirits, they had taught him these special songs to sing in time of crisis, danger, at the cross roads, near death. Big Bear then turned to his son. He told his son, "I had a very scary dream last night. It was about you, son." Big Bear told his young son, Horsechild, "This fall you will be sent home from the pile of bones [Regina today]. You will walk home all winter. You will have to cross the big Saskatchewan River in icy water, frozen ice on the edges."

Big Bear told his son, "My son, you are a strong man. You will make that trip, but it will take you all winter. We will be together for another three moons. The whitemen want you to freeze to death over the winter. But winter is a very kind spirit, also the story, winters are good spirits. The nights are also kind spirits. They will pity you. This winter spirit will keep you warm, and I will teach you how to survive."

(Chatsis, excerpt from his unpublished Horsechild manuscript)

I like writing about religion because religion is just a crazy thing. Through writing people could know that. So that is why I want to write it. I believe in Native Spirituality because you live it on a daily basis. You live and worship daily. I go to church all the time. Yes, I go to church all the time, but it's just to get to know people. I don't think any priest, or not even the pope, believes that there is a god because I don't think there is a god.

With Native Spirituality you do a lot of things. You have lots to thank for in this life. Maybe that's why the Indian got lucky and is getting all this whole thing for free. Now the white man was lucky to get this land for free. But now all the hard work they put on there, now the Indian is going to benefit from it for free. So it is no big deal for anybody. It just goes around. And the religious people…like the Roman Catholic church has too many big buildings right now. Too many big churches. They built great big churches because people would worship, they would believe that there was a god. But, less and less people, they don't believe in god anymore. And the priests don't have…nobody wants to be a priest anymore. And nobody wants to be a nun anymore either. So, they got these great big churches they don't know what to do with them.

I like writing about it because I think it was a stupid idea to begin with. And because they used to laugh at the Native people at the things that they did. You worship the tree, you worship the buffalo, you worship everything that was on earth, the trees, the rocks, the river, everything. So, that's your worship. The white religion only worships god, heaven, hell and the devil. And it is just faith. There is nothing there. You can never point out to anyone. No pope or bishop can ever point and say, "God is over on that side" or "God is over there." It is just all faith. It doesn't make sense.

What the Indian does is hoping to get well, and praying to get well, and you study your medicine, your herbs, and you try to make your life well. People used to laugh at us because we used to eat rabbits, and we ate gophers and we ate muskrats. But I have watched the white man, and I honestly didn't want to eat at the white man's house when I was a kid. I worked for this white man and I watched this chicken follow the cows that had been eating grain, and they were picking off from the droppings, you know, that was not digested I guess, or something. But that is what they were eating.

And when I look at a rabbit that is eating grass, and eating barks off little trees, and roots and things like that—that's healthy. That's the earth. That's what the earth provides. And the white man makes things that are going to taste good, but can be harmful. If you eat too much sugar, too many cookies—they're nice, cookies—you can buy a milkshake, you can make your own milkshake. You can buy pop, two litres of pop, and then you can buy a pail of ice cream, and at night you can be drinking this ice cream with pop, and have chips and cheezies and things like that with it, and be watching TV. But you're killing yourself, which is something I would never do, but I did at one time. I learned very quickly. I've lost eighty pounds.

Safety Deposit Box

"Where's your notebook, Albert?" I ask.
"I don't know."
"Is it in your car?"
"Probably."
"Why don't you get it?"
"I can't find it," says Albert.
"I don't doubt that. You have stuff piled up about four feet high in the back seat," I say.
"In winter I can just reach back and my gloves are on top of the pile."
"Usually you know where everything is?"
"Usually. But right now it is a little too full."
"What is all that stuff?"
"Papers, clothes. I don't have anywhere to put all that stuff at my apartment. It's like a safety deposit box."
"And your writing is in there somewhere?"
"Yeah. Somewhere. You got any paper?"
"Why aren't you using your notebook anymore?"
"This way if I lose anything, I don't lose it all. If I lose my notebook everything is gone. It is safer this way."

It is important to write down my stories because otherwise they would be lost forever, what I did, what I accomplished. It is very important to put these things down. By writing I can leave something. Otherwise they are lost forever. I can leave it as a legacy, or as something that I can be remembered by.

Writing is different than speaking. I think you have to be very honest with what you are writing because it is permanent. People are going to go back to you and look at what you wrote. Speech isn't permanent. When you write you have to justify it. It's like the court order they sent me. They have to justify what they wrote. And if I write back, and they threatened my life, it is going to go on record. It will be written. That is permanent. This is permanent. If I just said something, and if they just listened it wouldn't be permanent. They could say, "I don't think you said that. I don't remember exactly what you said, but I think you said this. I think you said that." That is the difference. I'm more careful when I write because I know it can have a recourse and come back to me.

When you write things down it allows you to keep part of the past. It is important depending on the situation because these events changed you. And what kind of life you accomplished. My life has changed. It has everything to do with writing. I want to be remembered for the things that I actually did. My mind changes as I see things better, the little secrets in life that you don't want to reveal. It gives me a sense of accomplishment. You realize what you've survived. You can realize your mistakes. You can adjust the course of your life. It gives you a sense of growth. People who don't write can never improve themselves because they can only go by what they remember. We're separate individuals, what I am and what I was. You have a course in life. Writing helps to join what I was and what I am.

Warren McDonald

Warren McDonald [pseudonym] is in his fifties, and has attended the Writers' Group for the last seven years, rarely missing a session. He and Albert are inseparable and always attend the Writers' Group together. As my research for the book continued, Warren became more and more involved with the study because of his interest in writing, and his friendship with Albert. I eventually decided to include Warren because his personal insights and writing are extremely powerful, heartfelt, and offer a deep insight into the development of self through the act of writing.

After each writing encounter, he returns home and types up his and Albert's writing on his computer. When he first started attending the group, Albert gave Warren a ride, and Warren agreed to type all of Albert's writing. They negotiated a barter system based on need and friendship. When we are ready to compile another book at the end of the year, he brings me a computer disk, containing all of his and Albert's writing.

When Warren first joined the Writers' Group, he was quite ill and didn't believe that he existed. In fact, Warren didn't believe that anyone or anything existed in the entire universe (which also didn't exist). In many ways the other members' acceptance of him, the resulting social camaraderie of the group and the act of writing helped Warren reconnect with himself and the rest of the world. This point will be touched on in the narrative, then developed as a central theme when I look at his writing in a later chapter.

I constructed Warren's narrative from transcripts of interviews, personal conversations, and extracts from his weekly writing. The words are his, but the narrative is structured as a literary work, weaving together the threads of diverse themes that Warren introduced in his writings and our interview sessions.

The Narrative of Warren McDonald: Writing from the Mind

I started coming to the Writers' Group about seven years ago. I was trying to get back into the world, part of what they called my socialization program. For almost ten years, I didn't go out of my apartment. I had a complex phobia and couldn't be around people. All I did was stay inside. The stress finally culminated in January of 1996 to the point where it was unbearable. I knew that I had to do something. My psychiatrist then referred me to a woman who was given the task of getting me into the mainstream of society. She recommended that I start attending various activities with the local Canadian Mental Health Association. I tried lots of different things, bowling, movies, coffee club, but I like the Writers' Group the best. Here I can express myself. I like that.

I first heard about the Writers' Group from a newsletter in 1996. When I first met Albert he talked a lot about writing and the group. He said that it was fun. The way it turned out was that I wanted an activity to replace swimming for the summer so I thought I would go to the Writers' Group for one or two sessions. If it didn't work out I would just quit, and if I liked it I would go all summer and then I would quit. I started going. I went to one session in July. I enjoyed it. I went to a second session. I kept on going. In the fall I said to Albert maybe I will have to quit now because it's getting dark and I can't see to walk. But Albert offered to drive me and I kept going. That was seven years ago. Seven years.

Now that I am in the group I like coming here to make friends. I can talk to people and socialize. If I do a serious piece of writing I can tell them about my life, or about something from my past. I like doing serious writing on things in my life from thirty or forty years ago, frustrating things from my teenage life. Then I feel better about it. I can get it off my chest. When I was locked up in the hospital, I only told them some of my problems. I really didn't tell them everything. I kept a lot of it secret and I always did that, even when they gave me sodium amatol to make me tell the truth. Here at the Writers' Group is the first time in my life that I'm really getting all the problems out in the open. I love that. Now I just like getting these things off my chest. I feel better and more relaxed. I go home after writing and I really feel good.

In my life I have had varying periods of extreme happiness and extreme sorrow. At the age of eleven I experienced the mental trauma of seeing all my family's possessions destroyed in a raging and blistering fire. In a few short hours the house and family store was completely gone. By midnight I remember myself and my mother standing in front of a pile of smoldering ashes, all that remained of everything my brother, my mother, my father and myself owned. We had very little insurance on the store and even less money in the bank. What would we do? This set the stage for a great mental struggle, which would last the rest of my life. We had to move to a new town and start over again.

In my life there has been a personal relationship with two towns, my hometown, and my teenage years' town. During the turbulent sixties, when I was a teenager, my place of residence was not where I spent my social life. That part of my life occurred in my town of birth, which was not far away. In one town I had "buddies." In the other town, the people despised the ground I walked on. In one town I was a likeable young boy. In the other town I was a professional "dope."

Things started to get worse. The first time I had an encounter with the Canadian justice system was in the sixties. It occurred at a time when I was a paranoid schizophrenic. At this time I had planned a perfect murder in which I was going to kill eleven people whom I had carefully picked from the community in which I lived. I had gone ahead and ordered a gun through mail order. My plans were to use the gun to kill some of the people and an axe from the neighbor's yard to kill the rest. However before the actual time came for the carrying out of the tragic event, I talked to a general practitioner who tried to have me admitted to the hospital. I refused admission. The next day I talked to a psychiatrist. On the basis of a fifteen-minute interview he issued a writ calling for my committal to a mental hospital. Approximately twenty minutes later the city police arrested me off the street and drove me to the city jail. They then took me into a little room where they made me partially undress and they frisked me. They then took me still without all my clothes to a cell. After a number of hours I was transported to the hospital by the RCMP. I am not sorry for having been put in the hospital. My qualm is: "Did the police have to arrest me off the street? Couldn't they have rather come to the house and made the arrest?"

Years later a psychiatrist told me how the Mental Health Act reads. It states clearly that if a psychiatrist and general practitioner agree that a person is a danger to society or themselves, they can be institutionalized. But he never explained why I was arrested in public, instead of at home. However, looking back at history from today, I realize now that the police did what they had to do. And to be honest or candid with myself, "I am not sorry for what they did."

I have always been able to regain my self-respect in life. With forced institutionalizations, I regained my self-respect. With paranoid schizophrenia, I regained my self-respect. With alcohol problems, I regained my self-respect. With shock treatment, I regained my self-respect. With trouble with the police, I regained my self-respect. With living in isolation, I regained my self-respect. With trouble in finding a job, I regained my self-respect. With feelings of negativism, I regained my self-respect. With emptiness in me, I regained my self-respect. With God's grace I hope I always continue to keep my self-respect. Because if we lose our self-respect, life is lost.

I enjoy writing now. I really enjoy it. I tried going to university after my second breakdown, and I got a chance to work on some interesting papers. Some marks were in the seventies, some in the sixties. But I didn't really enjoy it. I was with strangers all the time. Here at Writers' Group I'm with people I know good. I like that. I like having friends. I like having my stuff printed in a book at the end of the year. I enjoy that. I like that. It is kind of interesting.

I like the Writers' Group because it's my chance to get out into the world, which I never had before. And when I write I get a chance to get out into the world too. I can go out and explore new worlds, new avenues, new horizons. The Writers' Group is when I can go to a social outing. I like reading the writing out loud. Because if you are just going to read to yourself you won't enjoy the reading as much because no one hears you. If you can relate your story to other people it's always more fun. To me it's way more fun. If I had to do writing and just take it home I wouldn't enjoy it. I don't know. It is really important. I enjoy that because the writing can be discussed. The others can discuss it.

In high school I didn't write for some reason, and I didn't do that much reading. I didn't do much reading in high school. I did very, very little. I don't know why, I just never wanted to read that much in high school, just probably because of the way I felt. Also my, I have such a problem with my concentration. I couldn't concentrate in high school at all. After my attention problem came into focus in high school I couldn't concentrate on my studying. I tried to read a book, I couldn't read, I couldn't concentrate long enough. Because I never studied. I didn't do any studying in high school. That's another reason why I got low marks. Attention deficit disorder was part of it but also I made no attempt to study. In most of high school I didn't feel good enough, like mentally, to study so I never did any studying in high school. All I would do is I would go to school. I would be there from nine until three-thirty, and then I would come home and just sit in the house. The night before the exam I would go outside and sit behind a tree, and look over the book for maybe fifteen minutes. The next day I would go write the exam. Sometimes I passed, but sometimes failed.

Actually, I knew that from the time I moved the first time, since I was thirteen years old and on. I finished high school in June when I was nineteen. Then in November is when I had the first breakdown. That's when I was transported to the hospital. The things just kept on getting worse. I was aware the last year of school when I was in grade twelve that things weren't right. I knew things weren't right in my head just by all my thoughts. But I didn't want to admit to myself that I had a problem. I kept telling myself I'm normal, I'm normal, I'm normal. I kept telling myself that all that last summer of 1967. Kept saying I'm normal.

I didn't do that much writing as a kid. A little bit. I wrote some letters when I was a child. I wrote letters to my cousin in the United States, that kind of thing. But in high school I didn't do much writing. It wasn't until after I got out of the hospital and tried to go to university. University is when I started writing.

I think my writing skills are maybe about as good as they are going to get probably now. I don't know how much more they will improve. But of course if you don't do any writing your writing skills will get worse. I don't know how much they are going to improve now because now, I guess I'm not taking any more classes at the university. So it won't improve much more now. I don't know if they will keep improving with age or not. I like writing for fun, and just to keep my contacts open with the world. All these activities I go to keep my world open with society.

Because otherwise I would go back to the way I was thirty years ago when I had nothing. When I just sat in the house. If I don't keep my contacts open with society I will go back to the way it was when I was a teenager and I never went outside. I want to go out as much as possible. Keep me in touch with the world. Before I never went anyplace. I was paranoid at people. I was scared to go out. I don't know, now it's different. I go out in public even without Albert. It's way better than just sitting in the house. I feel good. Being alone is not fun and it just hurts you.

I do very little writing at home. I just go and type out the writings. I don't know. There is something about the Writers' Group. When I come here I feel like writing. I really feel like writing. At home I just don't feel in the mood. I like having friends at Writers' Group. I like that. I don't like it when many don't come. I like it when there are lots of people here. When I'm by myself I wouldn't write at all. I never had friends as a teenager. I want friends.

When I write I don't ever make notes before I write. I just write from my mind. Just what comes into my mind. Like at Writers' Group, I just write whatever comes to my mind. I just pretty much in my mind I plan what I am going to write and I go ahead and write it. When Jeff first gives a topic, all I do is think about ten seconds and then I sit down and start writing. Everything comes to me. I don't plan. It comes to me as I write. When I'm finished I don't make changes very often. Very rarely, rarely. Not too often. Not too many changes. I just leave it the way it is because to me it sounds good enough. It's the way I felt the way I wrote it. It's the way I felt.

Writing to me is a means of expressing my true personality or to borrow a term from the past, "freedom of self-expression." When I write my emotions "run wild" as well as my imagination. It releases my tensions and brings me pleasure in life. This is a method of communication that I have been using since I began writing seven years ago. I find that I am able to ventilate my feelings on such diverse issues as the creation of the universe, God, and mental illness.

For me talking about a subject doesn't help me much in writing. Being an impulsive person I do most of my best writing when I merely put pen to paper. Explaining my problems through the written word is an excellent method of resolving my problems. To me writing is the best method that I have found that truly reflects my inner personality.

The Writers' Group has really helped me. I get a chance to express myself. Writing for me is something I do to express my inner feelings, ventilate my emotions and give me a sense of personal satisfaction. I write whenever I am in the mood and want to achieve that sense of ecstasy that only writing brings.

Part III

Into the World

> "Do I contradict myself?
> Very well then I contradict myself
> (I am large, I contain multitudes)."
>
> Walt Whitman,
> *Leaves of Grass*

Chapter Five

At the Edge of Writing and Writing Theory

The narratives of four participants of the CMHA Writers' Group evoke the life worlds of these writers, and show the value they ascribe to writing. In constructing and writing the narratives, I presented the phenomenon of writing within the Writers' Group through a narrative way of knowing (Bruner, 1986). In this chapter, I examine the participants' writings to show the importance of writing in their lives, and the intense value they attribute to the act of writing. I include writing from all four of the participants, and focus on the value of writing in the expressive function. In presenting these ideas, I am exploring the phenomenon of writing through a "paradigmatic way of knowing" (Bruner, 1986). It is through the entwining of the narrative and paradigmatic ways of knowing that a deep understanding of the phenomenon of writing at the Writers' Group unfolds.

Social Aspects of Writing at the Writers' Group

For the writers at the CMHA Writers' Group, the social aspect of the sessions is extremely important. The significance of the social nature of the group, and its impact on the writing process, need to be explored in more depth. In his narrative, Brian compared the Writers' Group to the bar in the television show *Cheers*, an apt comparison because both locations provide a sense of home for the participants. The Writers' Group is a social venue for the writers, and provides them with camaraderie and entertainment. For many group members, the Writers' Group is an evening out, and the highlight of their social life. There is an element of acceptance and belonging that is central to the success of the group. There is, however, a crucial and extremely significant difference: the Writers' Group is not simply a place to socialize; it is also a place to work and learn and discover and play with language and ideas. In this chapter I also want to show how personal writing is actually a complex social and cultural act.

The value of the Writers' Group goes far beyond a simple social activity like bowling, or going for coffee or to a movie. The CMHA offers these activities in the form of clubs that are sometimes not as well attended as the Writers' Group. Several members have often communicated to me the value of the social aspects of the Writers' Group. Albert Chatsis says:

> I like the writing group. I have to work there. It's fun. It makes my brain work. And that is good because if you don't make your brain work it is going to die off. Like anything else, if you don't use it you lose it. Jeff's job at writing group is to get our brains working.

Albert's desire to think and learn and "make [his] brain work" provides insight into the true value of writing in his life. It is obvious that there is more at stake with the Writers' Group than its social significance. The writing itself is a major attraction. What is it about writing that provides such a powerful presence in Albert's life? In over eight years, Albert has never missed a session of Writers' Group despite storms and holidays. Like Albert, the rest of the writers enjoy the social aspect of the group, but it is the combination of the social atmosphere and the writing that draws them. People attend the Writers' Group to write.

Caroline also addresses the issue of the social attraction and significance of the Writers' Group:

> I like coming to the writing group. It is enjoyable and fun. People there are good. It is a special place because there is an atmosphere. It is a freedom. It's a unique place for me and I think that has a lot to do with the people there and the place where they are in their lives. The nonjudgmental. The total acceptance....With this writing group, there isn't the feeling of having to be perfect, having to be a certain way. There are no rules and regulations, and there is nobody trying to say, "Oh, that is not the way to do it," or, "You have to do it this way in order to get anywhere." There is nobody trying to be above anyone else.

Caroline's ideas are significant in trying to understand the importance of the social dynamics at the Writers' Group, including issues of power and acceptance. I asked her if I could simply teach the writers at the Writers' Group the "way to write" or show them the "proper way to do it." Caroline said that wouldn't work at all:

> No one would attend because there is no freedom of expression and that there is no depth to something that has no freedom....By providing acceptance and the atmosphere of freedom the writing is deeper, and it is real. It may not make total sense, and it may not be perfect, but it is real. It is the person's feelings, instead of just words on a piece of paper to look nice.

Brian maintains that the Writers' Group has become an institution, in that the individual members may change but the group keeps functioning. Brian says:

> The Writers' Group is a very good, strong group, and I believe it is taking on a life of its own. All we have to do is keep it moving and keep it stimulated and keep the writers coming. For a lot of them, the Writers' Group is the closest thing they have to a home. And that is important. It is a place where they feel welcome by everyone there. It is a place where they can express themselves without fear of ridicule, or embarrassment. I think it is one of the strongest institutions that I've ever been involved with, and I really feel good about being a part of it. It is a place where you can connect, and where people are not afraid to show a bit of intimacy, and also are not afraid to preserve a comfortable level of distance at the same time....They can just be who they are.

This simple idea of just being has significance on more than one level: they can just be who they are as humans and still be accepted, and yet their writing can express widely diverse and controversial ideas. I want to look at these ideas by looking at the importance of the group responses, or what Brian calls "feedback."

The importance of the social aspect of the Writers' Group pertains specifically to the value of the writing. Part of the success of the group is the immediacy it provides in terms of feedback, both to the writing, and the writers as persons. Brian says that as "a writer, you need feedback...The feedback has done wonders for my writing. The writers' group is a little closer, a little more intimate, and we can be a little more candid." Brian's statement is in agreement with much of the research on writing groups. Gere (1987) writes:

> In temporal terms, all writing groups provide response with an immediacy impossible in teachers' marginalia or reviewers' evaluations. Whether they receive comments from three individuals or a classroom full of people, writing group participants do not have to wait days or months to learn what others think of their work. In physical terms, writing groups reduce the distance between writer and reader. Even when responses take written form, authors operate in close proximity to an audience, enjoying opportunities to observe the effects of their work or to ask questions. (p. 3)

The Writers' Group provides the participants with an immediacy that is extremely significant to the writers. After each writing session, the writers take turns reading their writing aloud. Often the group will provide suggestions and encouragement immediately. At the very least, each member shares his or her writing with the rest of the group. It is this sharing that creates a sense of belonging.

The feedback provided by the Writers' Group often takes on an added significance that pertains to the identity of the writer. Brian says,

> Writing has always been such a very important part of who I am, and what I do, I can't divide the two. It identifies me in a very profound way, emotionally, intellectually and spiritually. My fundamental identity would be derived from a whole group of people that I interact with. But writing clarifies what it is for me. It adds clarity to my identity, and in this way, makes my identity much more secure.

This statement is illuminating for several reasons: it shows the value of collaborative work within the context of a writing group, and it also shows the relationship between the writing and a writer's perception of himself or herself. Brian suggests that writing clarifies his identity, and the feedback is an integral part of the process.

The social aspects of the Writers' Group, and the actual act of writing, work in conjunction with each other. Brian says:

> The way Jeff runs the Writers' Group, and the atmosphere of the group, both have great value. Probably it is easiest to see if I give you a comparison. I was involved in a few therapy groups in hospital, where they get people sitting around in a circle. Usually these groups are very much, and subtly, dominated by a leader. Although they are trying to be democratic, their autocratic nature does come through. And it very quickly degenerates into a game that everyone learns to play. We learn to play what the group leader wants us to say, and we learn to play the game the way the group leader wants us to play. We learn to say what she wants to hear, or what he wants to hear, and so we're certainly becoming compliant. In a group like this, it is dramatically different because it is all right to be different. It is all right to go off on your own tangent, if we don't go too dreadfully off one way or another. There is a lot more spontaneity in a group like this. We don't need a group leader to keep us focused on our concerns. We don't want to talk about our concerns necessarily, but if we become comfortable enough within this setting and feel unthreatened enough within an atmosphere like that, then the feelings and the concerns will come forth on their own, and they do.
>
> The social aspect of the writing group is entirely crucial. Without a warm and, in some cases, intimate social interaction, it's not very fulfilling. People enjoy being seen and they enjoy being heard, and they enjoy being recognized for something that they do well. And this builds. There are two interacting things. The social development and the communication development go hand in hand. One is not separate from the other. The communications factor supports the strength of the group socially, and the strength of the group socially improves their communication because it breaks down walls. The two are mutually supportive.

Brian's comments are a reminder of the complexity and relational nature of social systems. The Writers' Group achieves success because it operates on at least two levels simultaneously. The dominant activity at each session is writing, but the writing occurs within a significant social situation, and the two processes affect each other a great deal.

As I have mentioned earlier, we actively engage in the act of writing each week during our time together, and not just workshop writing that is done at home. The writing done each week is read aloud immediately, with each writer having the option to share what he or she has written. The sharing of the writing with the rest of the group is a key. Caroline says:

> Reading out loud is very, very, very important because it helps to lessen the fear for one thing. The fear of being laughed at, the fear of not being accepted. The fear of expressing in front of a group of people. And it stops you from being so...so alone. You're not alone anymore. And that is so vital because so many of those people are alone all the time. Even when they are around people they are alone because they are not accepted. There isn't any of that at the Writers' Group. There is no negative. People can talk about the negative but it isn't taken as negative. They're hurting and it's allowed. There is empathy here. There's not even sympathy; there's empathy.

The sharing of the writing is extremely important to the participants of the Writers' Group, as are their discussions of a variety of topics. Caroline says:

> It's the combination of everything—the writing, the reading, the sharing, and the acceptance because we are who we are...The Writers' Group is the one place that I have that I am just I. I don't have to play games. I don't have to pretend. I don't have to act....I can just be.

Caroline's comment is similar to Brian's idea of members being allowed to be who they are. There is a real sense of acceptance and trust within the group.

This book focuses on the value of the writing, but it is important to remember the relational importance of the social aspects of the writing group. Gere (1987) affirms this observation in the introduction of *Writing Groups: History, Theory, and Implications* when she writes:

> Perhaps the most significant commonality among writing groups appears in what they contribute to our understanding of what it means to write. Specifically, writing groups highlight the social dimension of writing. They provide tangible evidence that writing involves human interaction as well as solitary inscription. Highlighting the social dimension enlarges our view of writing because composition studies has, until recently, conceptualized writing as a solo performance. A variety of forces, ranging from aspects of intellectual history to social institutions such as copyright law, have contributed to the dominance of a solo-performance view of writing. (p. 3)

Writers do not work in complete social isolation; they are all part of a social context. Even if an individual writer chooses to be isolated, this decision is still social. The act of writing as an individual occurs within a complex, social web that ultimately influences the writing act, both directly and indirectly. As the social constructivists and cultural studies advocates have observed, writing is not an entirely personal act; however, neither can writing be defined as a completely social activity, based on a localized discourse community. Writing is created at the point of the dialectical tension between an individual understanding and a social understanding. How does personal writing engage and create meaning within the social web? The CMHA Writers' Group provides a territory for this exploration with a new focus on the social significance of expressive writing.

Chapter Six

The Writings of the Participants

In this chapter, I examine the writing of the four participants from the Writers' Group to explore the importance of writing for them as individuals. My purpose is not to analyze the writing for literary merit, though it often has literary value. Instead I use Britton's concept of writing functions, concentrating on the expressive function, to examine the value of personal writing, and to possibly re-conceptualize its significance and meaning.

I will italicize and indent all member writings to ensure that they maintain their own voice, separate from the body of my text. All writing by the members of the CMHA Writers' Group remains the property of the individual writers, and I have their permission to use it for this book.

Caroline and the Expressive Writing Function

Caroline's writing is a valuable site for exploring the meaning and value of expressive writing. When she first started to attend Writers' Group, she hesitated about joining. She felt her therapist and health care workers were pressuring her to attend the writing sessions. She also felt that she was different from the other writers because she was working and completely independent of social assistance. Now, after a few years of attending the group, she has become an avid writer and participant in the reading and sharing of writing. As outlined in the narrative that I created for Caroline, she comes from a very abusive past, an understanding that becomes relevant when looking at her writing. She has used her writing as a metaphorical place to examine her life. In the following piece of writing, she uses a poetic structure to examine pertinent elements of her life.

Life Missed

If people only knew the things they miss,
When violence has been their only kiss.
Trying hard to keep the things they do not want,
Never fighting for a life with open heart.
They do not see the freshness of a new born leaf,
The gentleness of water flowing in a brook,
Or, the warmth of sunshine in the blue, blue sky.
They see the barrenness of tree,
The muck within the water,
And the cloud of storm filled skies.
They see time without season,
Life without joy,
Bodies without soul,
So they destroy.
And think all the while
They are saving themselves,
Avoid feeling the good to avoid feeling the bad,
Kick around the good, so it knows the sad,
Never love, or laugh, for they may not win,
So, on goes the violence, over and over again.

(1999)

Though the writing is partially in what Britton would consider the poetic function (using language as a structure), the expressive function dominates. In her poem, Caroline writes about her abusive past to understand what caused the abuse, and presents a plea for others to understand what the abusers are missing in their lives. Caroline does not use the first person in this piece, although she is exploring issues from her past (personal communication, November, 2000). This distancing technique allows her to gain some perspective on the past. Britton (1979) maintains, "the expressive as utterance...relies on an interest in the speaker (or writer) as well as in what he has to say about the world" (p. 123). Caroline in verbalizing and documenting her ideas on paper negotiates both the meaning of her experience, and her sense of self in the world.

In another poem called *A Wish*, Caroline writes:

I sit in the night and think about, who?
I cry in my sleep for the closeness of two
To laugh, to run, to play in the sun,

To love in arms when the day is done.

But dreams can destroy all the beauty I feel
For I grab out and fight for the touch that is real
With my grabbing I push, with my fighting I lose,
For they think of me then as something to use.

If I could just start from the beginning again
Without masks or the sadness of all of the pain
Maybe then I could have what I so badly need
And maybe someone wouldn't feed their own greed.

Just to take in my hand for a second or two
Just to hold close to me for a moment or two,
A look in my eye without fear or the pain,
To see from my heart the most gentle domain.

Now, I sit in the night and I cry in my sleep
I dream of a life where no ugliness creeps,
I pray for a world that lets everyone see
A place where I've wished that we all could be.
                                                    (1999)

In this poem, Caroline acknowledges her past, and asks for a better future. Although she uses elements of poetic language with the couplet rhyme scheme (*aabb*), her writing operates for the most part in the expressive function. Caroline is actively engaged in making sense of both the past and a possible future, or what Bruner (1986) would call a "possible world." Again, Caroline solidifies ideas by putting them on paper. The writing helps her conceptualize her thinking. She organizes her ideas as she writes, and not beforehand. In an interview, Caroline gives us some insight into this process with a clear and beautiful description of writing in the expressive mode:

> Before you start writing there is a lot that stuff you don't know. Or you know it, but it is hidden. It is in a dark place inside of your brain and until you start to write it, you don't find it. A lot you don't want to find. I finally realized that there is a lot of stuff that I do not remember. I never want to remember. I don't have to. I know the initial thing—lived through it, felt the pain. I sure don't need to know the rest, you know? Our society teaches the opposite. They say I have to remember this and I have to remember that. Whenever I went for therapy it was the big thing to try and get me to remember every little detail of what happened to me, and once you remember then it is supposed to go

away. Well, no. Because once one thing has happened it can happen twenty-five times because it is the same thing happening. That's not the issue. The issue is what it does to you inside, what it takes from you. Your feelings. Who you are. The pain. But it's not the memory of what happened. It's the emotional pain that it does to you, because your body heals. It is your mind that retains. So there's this pain in there and there's ugliness in there and that is what somehow has to come out. In the writing, feeling is the big thing that is released even if the words don't make sense.

Caroline's comments provide insightful into the value of writing in the expressive function. Such writing doesn't simply express ideas and thoughts and feelings; it is also a means to conceptualize ideas and thoughts and feelings. Caroline says:

Writing is important because it is an expression. If you have only pain going on around you, if you have nowhere to release it, you become it. You become the pain, you become the anger, you become the frustration. If you shut down all parts of you that can hold on to the good, then you'll become the bad. Artistic ability is good, even if it comes out as painting a black hole because instead of holding that black hole inside, they're putting it outside.

You gain something when you write. I guess it's just a...you're not holding it inside. You're putting it out. You're letting it go. It's like before I had any counseling—the thoughts were in my head, so what would happen is that they would become jumbled. It's like a jigsaw puzzle that's been thrown in the air. You can't put the pieces together because, there are bits and pieces all over the place. So, then if you can talk about it, those bits and pieces, it's not what the other person is hearing, it's what you're hearing yourself. You're hearing yourself say it, so it's coming out and it's being put into place. And it starts to make sense, but if you can't talk about it, because there is nobody who will listen, or you're not allowed, then the writing of it does the same thing, it takes it out of the brain, and puts it into a perspective. It takes some of the pain, and it's like throwing it away. When you write and when it's on paper it's like throwing it away because it's outside of yourself now that you've expressed it.

Caroline provides us with an alternative view of the value of expressive writing from what is usually considered in writing practice and theory. The writing moves beyond the self, and, in Caroline's terms, is "thrown outside." In doing so, the writer can then more easily make sense of what has been expressed. If we begin to think of the self as more of a matrix rather than a unified entity, then the concept of moving the writing "outside" takes on a new perspective. Perhaps this movement beyond the individual helps explain the deep importance of the social aspects of the Writers' Group.

Ricoeur (1998) claims that much of Gadamer's work centres on "the opposition between alienating distantiation and belonging" (p. 363). Ricoeur's work with the idea of text and discourse can give us a different lens from that offered in Britton's view, and together the two can provide us with even greater depth. Ricoeur's ideas concerning text are exceedingly complex, but for my purposes have much relevance. Ricoeur claims that "text is much more than a particular case of intersubjective communication: it is the paradigm of intersubjective communication" (p. 363). If true, then the social aspects of the Writers' Group—the sharing of written texts within a space of mutual trust and respect, while still allowing for differences—become of paramount importance because of the intersubjective nature of texts. Ricoeur identifies five problematic themes regarding "the notion of text in view of that to which it testifies, the positive and productive function of distantiation at the heart of the historicity of human experience" (p. 363). His five themes are as follows:

> (1) the realisation of language as *discourse*; (2) the realisation of discourse as a *structured work*; (3) the relation of *speaking to writing* in discourse; (4) the work of discourse as the *projection of a world*; (5) discourse and the work of discourse as the *mediation of self-understanding*. Taken together, these features constitute the criteria of textuality. (p. 363)

Caroline's writing demonstrates the complexity and relevance of the concept of textuality. Writing, for Caroline, utilizes the notion of getting the ideas and feelings outside of herself as a structured work. Once the discourse exists as writing in a structured work, it can be objectified and more easily understood. Caroline often does not understand the meaning at all until after it exists outside of herself. Only after she writes can she make sense of things.

Caroline did a freewrite at one of the writing sessions that helped explain how she writes, and how her writing differs from speaking:

> *Thinking and Writing*
>
> I find there is little relationship with the surface mind and writing, if I want it to be good. The more I think the worse the writing is. I auto write, usually. It is not planned or tried for. It is just written. Once something is written, then there is a thinking process which goes to work.
>
> I used to blank out when I wrote and come to when I finished. It happened right up until I was in my twenties. From then on, I had a realization but it still just happened. I didn't write with thought. Even when writing essays in school. I never outlined or figured out. I would read the book and then just write. My novel, I didn't even think about or figure out what I wanted to say. I just sat down one day and three months later I had over 500 pages. I always believed my writing was given to me, as if it was not attached to me. Maybe this is true. At times, I feel I do not deserve to have it. (February 13, 2001)

During one of our interviews, Caroline mentioned that when she wrote her novel she was unable to stop writing: "Suddenly there were these thoughts going through my head. It wasn't a thought process. It was just writing." Caroline feels the need to externalize her ideas and feelings through the act of writing; she then makes sense of her ideas after she writes.

Caroline uses expressive writing to make sense of her place in the world, and her writing is a form of negotiation. In the following piece of writing, she writes in the third person, using the persona of Dora, to express her difficulty reading when she was a child.

The Text Book

Dora sat quietly at her desk with a reader in front of her. Slowly she opened the pages and looked at the words. "What do I do now," she thought. "Each time I look at the words they run together." Each time she was asked to read for the class, she broke out in a sweat. Each time she tried, she cried.

Day by day, not letting herself give up, she worked on it. When she sat alone, with everything quiet, she worked on it. It came slowly but as she got through each page she realized something very important. Even though she had a problem reading the words, she knew what she read. Never having to read it twice, she understood what was written on the pages. She could write on what she read and explain it well, but most of all Dora could write in a fluent and easy to read way.

As she grew up and as she learned more and more she realized with every handicap there is a counter ability. If we work with it, learn what they are, we can accomplish many things. Most of all, Dora learned, no one is any more wise or unwise than anyone else. We are all equal in our own right. We are all capable of being who we are for who we are. And who we are is ok and should be. (July 28, 1999)

In her writing, Caroline constantly negotiates a sense of self in relation to others and the world, often by exploring issues and experiences from her past.

Caroline's largest writing project so far has been her 438-page semi-autobiographical novel, *The Haunting Eyes*. She gave me the entire novel after Writers' Group one evening and said to read it if I had time. I was teaching several classes at the time and told her that I was incredibly busy, but that I would do my best to read it when some time opened up.

A few months later, Caroline wrote me a letter stating that I was just like all the other men that she had known and that I had lied to her when I had said I would read the novel. While I had managed to read half the book, I had not found the time to finish it. I immediately called her and after a lengthy conversation she understood that I had not lied to her about wanting to read it, and that I had truthfully been too busy to finish it.

I mention this incident because it shows the tremendous value that Caroline places on her writing. Although she probably wrote the book mainly for herself, she still felt strongly about my reading it and giving her feedback.

The novel traces a young woman who is running away from an abusive husband. The plot line mostly concentrates on meeting a new man, and coming to an understanding of her past experiences. Although it is always difficult to trace a writer's literary roots, it is probably safe to say that Caroline based some of the literary structures on romance novels with similarities in character development, plot points, writing style, and dialogue.

She wrote the novel in the third person using Wanda as the main character. Caroline begins the novel from the point of view of Matt, the secondary character:

> Matt walked slowly toward the front door of the apartment block. For some reason, he felt uneasy about this visit. He was an insurance investigator and he had, in his briefcase, a certified cheque, which he was delivering to a client. If the recipient had not contacted the agency by now, chances were she did not know what it was about. He had been working on the case for many months now and had almost given up finding her. His mind went over all the possibilities of what he would say; how he would approach her? (Murphy, 2000, p. 1)

Matt, an insurance adjuster, is delivering a check from a life insurance policy, which her husband had taken out before he was killed in a car accident. The husband, of course, was abusive in the past, and his death provides Wanda with the opportunity to deal with her abusive past. Caroline begins the novel from the secondary character's point of view, a technique that may be another form of distantiation. In an interview, Caroline had said that writing about this subject matter from the main female character's point of view was too difficult and painful for her to gain any perspective. Wanda, the main character, is portrayed as a strong woman:

> Matt couldn't believe the differences he was witnessing, from the withdrawn frightened woman to this easy going person who was ushering him into her home as if she knew him, talking openly about what? There was something unusual about her, something strong now. (p. 3)

The novel has several melodramatic characteristics including a dream ending; however, the focus of this discussion is the value of the writing for Caroline. Writing the novel seems to have resolved several conflicts for her. Near the end of the novel she writes:

> The morning came early to Wanda. She rose and began to look through the pages of her book. It was finally finished and it was good. Somewhere inside she felt an ache. Why? She knew. It was done and life was as it was. It was only a dream, the book. It was time to let go. (p. 436)

Caroline ends her novel with the main character, Wanda, realizing that she is alone, yet in the next month her two children will visit.

Writing the novel had extreme importance for Caroline. She said she couldn't write the novel in the first person because it was too painful. Although she changed certain things in the book, she said "there are a lot of events that are my life. That book scares me." Because of the closeness of the experience to the actual writing, Caroline had great difficulty making changes to the novel after she had finished because the novel is "a lot about my life. It would be like cutting pieces of my own life, or cutting out pieces of life." Caroline's writing, and her comments, demonstrate how seriously many writers value expressive writing. Her comments also provide insight into the difficulty some writers encounter when asked to revise or edit their work. The writing, so close to self, becomes extremely difficult to see as an artifact that can be manipulated. This acknowledgement of the importance of writing to the conceptualization of self, perhaps gives educators a slightly different perspective regarding the complexity of the revision process.

Brian Borley and Expressive Writing

Brian Borley, the most prodigious of all the writers who have attended the Writers' Group, rarely misses a session, and does a great deal of writing at home. He also covers the most genres in his writing. Since joining the Writers' Group, Brian has written two novels, a number of short stories, innumerable essays, letters to the editor (many of which have been published in provincial newspapers and newsletters), poems, lifewritings about past experience and family, and has created his own Web page. Using Britton's writing functions as a structural guide, it is clear that Brian utilizes all three functions. Although most of his writing begins in the expressive function, Brian's personal writing often moves to the transactional and the poetic functions, a very complex process to understand.

Much of the writing Brian completes at the Writers' Group begins with freewriting. Like most of the writers, he simply starts writing, and in the act of writing discovers what it is he wants to communicate or express. The freewriting is not a superficial act for Brian—much of the resulting writing has great depth. The freewriting activity is extremely complex and works on several levels simultaneously. Like many of the other writers at CMHA, Brian is able to conceptualize ideas and discover meaning during the act of writing. He is also involved in a social group that has real value to him, and he is no longer isolated as a writer. The freewriting that occurs at the CHMA Writers' Group is a social activity, as well as an individual act. Elbow (2000) has recently come to see this social aspect as important to the success of the activity:

> Freewriting is always private—by definition, for the sake of safety. But I have come to feel an intriguing link between freewriting and sociability because I so often do this private writing in the company of others—with a class or a workshop. Thus true freewriting "by the book," never pausing, has come in certain ways to feel like a companionable activity: one sits there writing for oneself but hears other people's pens and pencils moving across the paper, people moving in their chairs, sometimes a grunt or sigh or giggle. The effect of using these conditions for freewriting (however private) is to contradict the association of writing with isolation. An even more important effect is the palpable sense of "Look at all these people putting words down on paper without agony. If they can do it, well so can I!" (p. 120)

The social aspects of the freewriting activity result in an interesting situation—the writers are able to express their ideas and feelings in a social situation. They have immediate feedback to the writing and this immediate response, as well as the support and encouragement, drives them to write more.

Brian also writes a great deal at home, working on essays, short stories, and poems, often germinated from ideas that came out in the writing activities and discussion topics from the Writers' Group sessions. For Brian, the writing activity is now a way of life.

Most of the writing Brian completes at Writers' Group each week has been compiled in the year-end books that we publish for the writers. It is difficult to make generalizations and assumptions about his writing because of the vast scope of topics and genres. It is, however, valuable to examine some of the writing to gain insight into the value that writing has in his life. Years ago, Brian wrote a poem that illustrates his use of the expressive function to explore meaning in his life:

> *Madness*
>
> I have known love, unfettered by deceit.
> the dreams of childhood;
> butterflies and hummingbirds;
> the dreams of polka-dot ponies against a soft black sky.
>
> And I have known madness;
> The madness of a vision where Jesus, Mohammed, Moses, and Buddha with Gandhi and a gentle Cree took a communion of peace and life.
>
> The madness that a child I loved and lost to death should rise to life within the will and consciousness of the great spirit who rules all.
>
> I saw the vision of the Cree; my brothers and sisters; buoyant and filled

*with laughter where the buffalo lounged in green pastures; fulfilled in
the abundance of life.*

*Such things are surely the stuff of madness,
and surely I am mad;
But fear not my brothers and sisters.*

*Mine is a gentle madness.
Not the madness of the Enola Gay.*

(Fall, 1994)

This poem is a good example of the complexity of Brian's use of writing. Here he explores ideas of love and madness, and an experience from his life that he is trying to understand ("The madness that a child I loved and lost to death should rise to life"). What is perhaps most interesting is Brian's ability to move from the purely personal level of his own immediate experience to larger social issues like religion and violence. The last two lines of the poem act as a bridge between the personal and the social: "*Mine is a gentle madness. / Not the madness of the Enola Gay.*" The meaning of madness and love and loss is not simply an individual concern; it is also a communal or social concern. Brian's writing operates on a similar level of complexity—individual experience kindles a social response in that the writer is trying to make sense of the experience in larger social terms. The self, instead of being isolated, is part of a larger social network. Faigley's (1992) concern with the limitations of expressive writing can largely be accommodated within a new perspective of the self. In this sense, the self is not a separate entity onto itself, but instead is part of a complex matrix of the individual and the social.

Writing has traditionally been seen as a means of communication between people—a way of conveying or transporting an idea. Many of the process-composing theorists (Macrorie, 1988; Murray, 1984) have examined the use of personal writing as a means to explore or discover what the writer thinks or feels about an idea or issue or concept. Writing—expressive, personal, reflexive—is seen as a means for the writer to make sense of something. Usually this sense-making has been seen as individual exploration of the self, using "language that is 'close to the self'" (Britton et al., 1975, p. 90) as a means to express those thoughts. Brian's writing helps show a limitation with this viewpoint: the self is not an isolated entity. It is instead part of a complex social network. Everything is relational, and meaning is part of a larger matrix.

In the fall of 2000, Brian enrolled in a university class on computer programming. After a few days of the class, he noticed that he was becoming extremely agitated, and because of his history of mental illness triggered by stress, he decided to drop the class. Although he talked about the situation with his family, and with me, and probably his doctor, he only really understood the situation after he had written about it. Brian says, "It was a bit of blow to my ego, when I had to withdraw from my computer class, and I resolved it. But I don't think I could have resolved it without writing it down, and actually looking at it. It gave me a little distance. It gives me a little greater edge, a little greater objective edge. Usually, I believe, some of my best writing has come about when I'm trying to employ writing to resolve some of the minor conflicts, or some of the minor crises in my life."

Brian used writing to sort out his crisis involving the computer class, yet his writing was not purely in the expressive function. Brian was able to fictionalize the experience, using the incidents in his life to drive the story. He says, "I wrote this story. It was extensively autobiographical, but actually it dealt with the life of a boy who grew up about the same time that I did. In the end, he reflected on the attitudes his father had taken when he was faced with a similar crisis." Brian's use of language is extremely complex in this piece of writing. He used writing to objectify his experience and in doing so understood the experience more clearly.

Yet Brian did not stay in the personal, expressive or reflexive function of writing. He fictionalized the experience in a very complex and indirect way, almost as if he internalized the affective aspects of the experience and created a narrative structure to explore those feelings.

"The Builder" opens with the following paragraph:

> *It was 4:30 a.m. and Charles was having his coffee a bit early, but not especially early for him. He had retired early, shortly after the news cast that ended at 10:30. His wife Darlene had all but given up on trying to have him sleep later. He got out of bed when he woke, dressed in the dark, so as not to wake his companion of forty years, or his son, Christopher. Christopher was invaluable in the shop in the basement. A harsh word between them never seemed to arise.*

This paragraph parallels Brian's own life almost exactly. He is married, and has a forty-year old son living at home. He has simply changed the names. He draws other details in the story from his life and experience, and in many ways, he is simply using personal experience to add descriptive detail to the story. Later in the story, he mentions Charles' love of music, his projects involving the building of stereos and speakers, and descriptions of his family. All these details correspond to Brian's real life. Yet he is attempting to create a work of fiction. In Britton's terminology, Brian is trying to move from the expressive function to the poetic function (Britton et al., 1975). The move is less than complete, and because of that it gives an opportunity to perhaps trace what Brian was trying to do, and what value this type of writing has for him.

Later in the story, Brian has the character Charles listen to music and read a magazine:

> His mind was not fixed on the articles on child slavery with much intensity. An issue like child slavery could still raise the hackles of the old man, since as a retired teacher, he had a real and very close attachment to children. The word "Nike" filled him with a thinly subdued rage. This week-end he thought it would be a delight to walk in protest carrying a sign reading, "Buy Nike! Support Slavery."
>
> The "Global Economy" which Charles saw as an initiative by the transnational corporations to become wealthy on the products of slavery of one form or another, detracted from the overall harmony in his life.

Again, Brian is using his own life as a model for the character of Charles. He uses the act of listening to music and reading to explore social issues in the story. The story does not work in a plot-line context with a resolvable conflict; instead the story functions as an inner exploration and expression of thought and belief. Brian continues:

> He wondered if the scum who pursued wealth on the back of slaves had ever seen a rose, or been moved by a haunting melody. He seriously wondered if a rose, or a melody, or the majesty of the setting sun ever moved them from their singular vanity and narcissism. Slavery was the ultimate measurement of life, the measure that dictated that a slave was less human than the follower of crass materialism.

In the story, Brian moves from the personal to the social. Brian has the character, Charles, think about slavery, a social concern, and relate it to modern capitalism. Brian is using his own life to measure and gain perspective. In many ways, he is simply echoing his own beliefs and ideas, and using the character of Charles to give them voice. I confirmed this observation when I spoke with Brian about the story, and how he used the act of writing it to cope with the mental crisis.

Donald Murray (1991) claims that all writing is autobiography. Brian obviously used his life experience to create the story, moving from expressive writing to poetic writing. Why, for instance, didn't Brian simply write about his frustration regarding the computer class? Why distance the emotional impact by creating a fictional account?

In the final few paragraphs of the story, Brian writes:

> *He was sitting back in his chair, while the strains of Dvorak's New World Symphony lulled him, and gave him respite from his anger.*
>
> *His wife, Darlene, approached him in a coquettish manner, and pulled the headphones from his head. She asked him what he wanted for breakfast. He saw Christopher emerge from his bedroom in his housecoat, and ask if anyone needed the bathroom before he showered.*
>
> *Charles felt truly pampered, a feeling he enjoyed. After breakfast of French toast and ham, the three of them walked the streets and trails on the edge of the city where the birds sang, and the sun was a warm blanket of comfort. They spoke little. The strains of music still echoed in Charles' head. It was a glorious day as it awakened.*

In terms of the story, Brian resolves Charles' inner conflicts by simply describing a domestic scene of simple tranquility.

How did Brian move from the expressive function to the more abstract poetic function? First of all, Brian reads widely, and this knowledge facilitates the movement of the personal into the poetic. He also taught school for a number of years, and is quite aware of the acceptable format for essays and letters. The move from the expressive to the transactional or poetic is actually very complex. It is not, as many theorists have interpreted from Britton's work, necessarily a natural progression or growth (see Minock, 1994). Brian's story "The Builder" is not completely successful as a short story, or a work of fiction. It lacks a clear plot. There is little character development or conflict. The story is basically static and instead describes a domestic scene that contains much love and tranquility, which are qualities Brian felt he needed to explore to understand and get through the mental crisis of dropping the computer class.

On the other hand, as a piece of expressive writing, the story is extremely successful. What is of theoretical interest is how Brian's story shows the possibility of how it might be possible, in Britton et al's. (1975) terminology, to move the writing from the expressive function to the poetic. This is a very complex shift in thinking for the writer, and it is likely that in this case the movement is incomplete. Hemley (1994) mentions the difficulty of this problem in *Turning Life into Fiction*: "You must remember that you're writing fiction, not biography. Fiction, by its nature, involves transformation" (p. 71). What is the transformation, and how does it function? Why does Brian's writing not work completely as a piece of fiction, or what Britton would call writing in the poetic function? Fiction requires the ability to operate in what Britton calls the spectator role. Brian is still very much in a participant role, and that is what makes his writing less successful in terms of a short story in the poetic function. By shifting to a more speculative role, Brian would gain some distance from the experience and thereby see it more clearly.

Brian Borley has recently created a home page on the Internet called "Grampa's Website." He has created his Web page in a magazine or newsletter format that reflects his interest in literary forms. Each edition of the web page begins with a brief letter introducing the specific "issue," a table of contents, and several organized sections each containing letters, articles, essays, or photos. The Web page always begins with Brian's welcoming letter in which he updates each issue of the newsletter. The voice in these letters is that of Grampa Borley. A sample of one of the letters is as follows:

Grampa's New Letter

August came in hot and has stayed hot. In July, Grandma and Grampa spent a week in Winnipeg with our little one, a dear wee girl of two, perfect in every way.

Several new items will be found in this month's issue. There is also little news, since we have battened down the hatches against the heat, and have stayed close to home.

The new babies, including the one born at one pound four ounces, are doing just fine. (She is now a whopping eleven pounds.) The children next door are still a big ray of sunshine in Grampa's life. They enjoy the paddling pool in their back yard. The oldest graduated from Playschool. With her mortar board, big smile, and flashing eyes, she was the most gorgeous of the graduating class.

Bye for now.
Grampa Borley

(From Web page Volume 2, Issue 8, August, 2001)

Brian has organized the contents of the Web page into a series of sections, the contents of which are as follows:

Letters and Announcements
Stories Old and New

> On the Lighter Side
> Family Life
> Poetry Selections
> Social and Political Issues
> Personal and Spiritual Development
> Technical and Construction Projects
> The Mental Health Community

Each of these sections contains a series of related articles or essays or stories organized around a dominant theme. Each section shows a different aspect of Brian's vast interests, and in doing so provides a different facet of Brian's composite "Web identity." *In Life on the Screen: Identity in the Age of the Internet*, Turkle (1995) notes that:

> On the Web, the idiom for constructing a "home" identity is to assemble a "home page" of virtual objects that correspond to one's interests. One constructs a home page by composing or "pasting" on it words, images, and sounds, and by making connections between it and other sites on the Internet or the Web. (p. 258)

Brian's Web-identity, or what Turkle calls the "home identity," centres on the larger persona of Grampa Borley. Brian's use of a home page is an interesting site to consider his writing. As Turkle has noted, "one's identity emerges from whom one knows, one's associations and connections. People link their home page to pages about such things as music, paintings, television shows, cities, books, photographs, comic strips, and fashion models" (p. 258). Brian, through his posting of writing and the series of links, provides us with an insight into the value of writing as a means of constructing the self, not as an entity, but as a multiplicity. Turkle notes that "home pages on the Web are one recent and dramatic illustration of new notions of identity as multiple yet coherent" (p. 259).

Turkle's identification of Web pages as illustrations of "multiple yet coherent" selves gives us a vehicle to better understand Brian's writing. Brian uses writing to explore and discover his thoughts and ideas on a vast array of topics. In doing so, he is creating a sense of self. The Writers' Group provides him with a site to explore this construction of self through the writers' experiences and created texts.

Albert Chatsis and Expressive Writing

Albert Chatsis, the longest participating member of the Writers' Group, is a Native American male living in a predominantly white culture, who writes from a cultural and social perspective that is the result of a complex life of experience, of a self engaged in a world of others. He is not an isolated and fixed entity; instead he is in a constant state of change and revision. He is also moving, in a cultural sense, from a predominantly oral tradition to a world of writing. What language is closest to the self? What is natural for Albert? These are very complex issues. Albert's writing and his experience at the Writers' Group can provide a slightly different perspective of expressive writing, and what value it has to a writer.

Over the past ten years, Albert Chatsis has written on hundreds of topics at the Writers' Group. He likes to write about a variety of topics because he says it makes his brain work, and he really values that experience. Albert loves stories. He loves to listen to stories, and more importantly, he loves to tell stories. He is a member of Toastmasters, which requires members to compose speeches on very little notice. He loves the challenge of speaking and relating a story to others.

He writes mostly in a language that is close to his speech. He also uses language to discover what he thinks, and to express his feelings and thoughts. His writing probably would be considered as personal or expressive, but it is certainly not limited to that function. His writing is frequently poetic, and contains complex information that is conveyed to an known audience. Albert's writing is an interesting site to explore the value of writing for an individual, and more specifically, to consider the true value of expressive writing for a writer.

The first book of the CMHA Writers' Group, *Communal Solitudes*, was completed in 1993. Albert's first writing selection in that book, "North American Native Spirituality," provides a good starting point to explore the complexity of what it means to write in the expressive function. In the first three paragraphs, Albert writes:

North American Native Spirituality

> I watched my own grandmother killed by a bad medicine man. This type of spirituality and knowledge can be used to kill people or heal people.
>
> Once I was very sick, in fact near death. I was so sick I blacked out. When I came to, both my grandparents were rubbing me, and placing wet cloths all over me. There was also a strange smoke smell and they got me sitting up to give me a drink of herbal medicine. I don't really know what was wrong with me, but the next day I was playing outside in good health.
>
> But my grandmother was not that lucky. The way it went was my grandmother had stole her best friend's husband away from her, and really hurt her best friend's feelings. She hurt her so much that her friend asked an old male friend to kill her with this native spirituality. (September, 1993)

The Writings of the Participants 123

In this piece of writing, Albert describes an extremely important experience for him. Butler and Bentley (1997) would consider this writing a good example of lifewriting because Albert is using his own life experience to focus a piece of writing that clearly has meaning for him. He is using the writing to discover what he remembers and thinks and feels about past experience. He is using the writing, and the act of writing, to gain an understanding of the experience. John Dixon (1975) would consider this writing to be "personal," while Janet Emig (1971) would consider the writing to be "reflexive." James Britton would consider this writing to be expressive because Albert is using language "that is close to the self" (Britton et al., 1975, p. 90) to explore experience that is important to him. Albert appears to use writing as a means to explore and discover (p. 82), and the writing "has the functions of revealing the speaker, verbalizing his consciousness, and displaying his close relation with a listener or a reader" (p. 90). In the scholarly community, Albert's writing could be categorized as "lifewriting," "reflexive writing," "personal writing" or "expressive writing." It is important to keep these theoretical frameworks in mind when we look at the value of writing to Albert.

In his narrative, Albert Chatsis mentions the need to "expose" the past and to "release inside pressure." He says, "If I wrote them [the stories] out and exposed them to others I could let go." The act of writing is an act of release for Albert, which becomes a means to understand his life.

Albert concludes "North American Native Spirituality" with these three paragraphs:

> Today, thank the Great Spirit the Native spiritual beliefs are coming back, while the other churches are fragmenting into many different groups, not well understood, practically fighting amongst each other. Is this the wishes of God, the Great Spirit, or the devil?
>
> It makes me sad to be in the middle of these money hungry churches that, I partly believe, had brainwashed me not to believe in the good parts of Native spirituality.
>
> I pray to the Great Spirit every night to make me see the right way to live and I do my very best to be peaceful, kind, and understanding—with the very little or limited mental ability I now have. I just pray that we can all understand each other and respect each other as human beings.

Albert is expressing his feelings, ideas, and thoughts about those past experiences, and making connections to the present. In other words, he is negotiating the meaning of those experiences and integrating them into a sense of identity. He is using language through the act of writing to construct a sense of meaning to his life. Allen (2000) maintains that "personal essays provoke reflections:

Who am I? What is my experience? And finally, what is its meaning?" (p. 282). What occurs at the Writers' Group is an exploration of self and experience through language.

But one must open up the concept of what it means to write for the self in terms of expressive language. An individual does not exist in isolation; therefore, much meaning-making involves the negotiation of the self with others. Albert often writes about social issues. This writing has great personal meaning for him. The following poem is an example:

Poverty

Poverty means, to some, having less material goods or money.

Happiness is another thing all together.
Good health is completely different also.

To be poor, you can still have all of these,
only less of the material things and money.

Freedom is the most important thing to me personally.
Too much control, or just someone always looking over my shoulder
Can drive me into being physically sick.

This can make my mind weak,
And a weak mind can make my whole body
less functional, weak, and sick—or die.

(Spring, 1994)

In this piece of writing, Albert explores issues of a self in society to gain personal understanding of how he "fits in." Although the writing is personal, he attempts to explore a deeply social issue. The writing illustrates that one cannot separate the individual from the cultural and social context in which he or she is embedded. Writing is not simply an individual act, even if one uses the framework of Britton's expressive writing; writing is also a cultural and social act.

When Albert has free choice about writing topics, he likes to write about Native spirituality, the traditional Native way of life, religion, politics, justice, and social issues. Another dominant interest in his writing concerns his adopted father, Horsechild, the son of Big Bear, the famous Cree chief who has been the subject of many historical and fictional books and accounts.

Writing about Horsechild is extremely important for Albert; in fact, he considers finishing the Horsechild story the most important thing in his life. He grew up listening to his adopted father tell stories about the historical past, Cree beliefs, native spirituality, history, and his father, Big Bear. Albert says that he has a hundred stories in his head and he wants to write them all down eventually.

Albert says, "It is very important to put these things down. It should be exposed, the way this country was built. By writing I can leave something. It is important to me." Albert knows that writing is important for him, but he also feels a responsibility to "expose" the past and record it as a permanent record. In other words, though Albert is writing for himself, he is also concerned with others, and clearly communicating ideas and experiences to others.

What is it about writing the story about Horsechild Albert finds so important? When asked this question, Albert said that Horsechild was brave and honest and his feat of walking over five hundred miles in the middle of winter to get home after the trial of Big Bear accomplished something that was beyond any other human being. Albert's admiration for Horsechild is without question. But why write about Horsechild rather than just tell people about it? Albert says, "I have been writing the book for several years. I want to publish it so others can learn the true story. The other books on Big Bear and Horsechild are full of lies. People need to know what has happened. Through my writing they could know that." By writing the Horsechild story, Albert realizes he is creating a permanent record for others to refer to at any time. In other words, the writing becomes a cultural artifact.

There are several ways to look at Albert's writing in the Horsechild narrative. Albert's writing could be construed as expressive, using writing close to the self to discover what he thinks and feels about experiences that are important to him. The writing could be seen as transactional because he designed it to communicate with others and even persuade them of a particular viewpoint. According to Albert, his book sets out to tell the truth, and he feels a need to inform others. Finally, the writing is often poetic in its structure and its playful use of language. Probably the best starting point is to consider what the writing is doing for Albert. In other words, what value does the writing have for Albert?

Albert considers the Horsechild story the most important thing in his life. In the story he is trying to make sense of his father's life and the historical meaning of that life. But Albert does much more in the writing of the Horsechild narrative. He is also trying to make sense of his own life, and how it connects with his father and the historical past. Albert is trying not only to express his self; but also to discover his self in relation with others, and his place in the world.

The Horsechild story as a narrative moves forward in time, for the most part chronologically, to retell Horsechild's experience at the time of the Northwest Rebellion in 1865. Horsechild was the youngest son of Big Bear, one of the principal figures in what became known as the Frog Lake Massacre. After the Rebellion ended, Big Bear and Poundmaker were imprisoned and put on trial. After the trial, Horsechild walked home in the middle of winter. This Odyssey-like adventure forms the heart of the narrative. Albert also takes small tangential movements from the central plot of the narrative to explore such social issues as race, politics, justice, Native spirituality, and religion.

Albert writes the narrative in the third person for the most part, although Albert often will "enter" the narrative in the first person to comment on the incidents. In the writing, he actively engages in making meaning. At one point in the narrative, Albert interjects and writes a section he calls "Very Important":

> I will leave Horsechild in the big canvas tent for a while. It is absolutely necessary for me to tell the honest truth. With tears in my eyes I pray to all the forces of nature, both in spirit form, to guide me and make me not forget Horsechild's words in desperation times. Because I know at my age, I have read many a version written about Big Bear and what a bad Native he was. Here is the true viewpoint by Horsechild about his father and his own life.

Albert's narrative about Horsechild actually works on a number of levels. He chronologically tells, or presents, the story of Horsechild and what he experienced as a young man. He also comments on the story as it progresses through time. For the dominant thread of the Horsechild narrative, Albert bases the plot line on Horsechild's own telling of the story to Albert when he was a child. Albert became the next link on a chain of recipients of an oral tradition. As Albert says:

> With the Horsechild story, I just follow what he [Horsechild] said. I don't correct it or make changes. I write the story in order of what happened. I don't change it because I'm not making up the story. I'm telling the story the way it was told to me. If it is wrong, if it doesn't make sense, I'll leave it. I'm repeating the story as it was told to me. My grandfather would never mislead me. I trusted him one hundred percent. I'm writing a true story. There is no fiction on it. There is nothing that I've read from anyplace else, from anybody else. I've read a lot about Big Bear and Horsechild and everybody else, but I just erased that from my head. Because I didn't think it was true, and because I don't believe it.

Albert uses narrative to create meaning in his life. Buford (1996) claims "stories protect us from chaos....We have returned to narratives—in many fields of knowledge—because it is impossible to live without them...They are a fundamental unit of knowledge, the foundation of memory, essential to the way we make sense of our lives" (pp. 11-12). Albert, by writing the stories of Horsechild he learned as a child, not only validates his sense of self, but also validates his cultural and social background. When Albert writes the stories he learned from the predominantly oral tradition of his childhood, he is "fixing" the meaning for himself and others. Is this shift from an oral tradition to a written tradition part of assimilation into Western culture, or simply an acknowledgment that the stories of the oral tradition would end with his death? Albert has told me that he thinks there would be no one to carry the stories for him, and has mentioned that he writes for his grandchildren and great-grandchildren. The expressive function is the matrix for Albert to create a narrative that helps him understand both his past and his present situation, personally, socially, historically and culturally.

Warren McDonald: The Man Who Wrote Himself into Existence

I explore the writing of Warren McDonald [pseudonym], the fourth member of the Writers' Group, to show how powerful the act of writing can be in the life of an individual writer. With this examination, I want to show that writing has other uses beyond communication with others or as a tool "to get things done" (Britton et al., 1975, p. 88). Warren used expressive writing to explore and discover who he was, and link it to the person he now considers himself to be.

Warren basically wrote himself back into existence at the Writers' Group. As a young man, Warren had a psychotic episode that involved a violent fantasy. After relating this fantasy to his psychiatrist, the information was forwarded to the RCMP and he was arrested and committed to a psychiatric hospital, where he was badly treated and abused. Upon release, Warren lived in isolation, and did not leave his apartment for over nine years. About six years ago, Albert eventually talked him into attending the Writers' Group; Warren has not missed a session since.

For his first two years at Writers' Group, Warren would write on every topic, and participated fully. The atmosphere at the Writers' Group was relaxed and, though somewhat shy, Warren began to enjoy himself; however, both in conversation and in his writing, he was not fully engaged. He would inevitably end each conversation and piece of writing with a brief statement about how nothing matters because nothing really exists, including himself.

The following examples are the last lines from several of his writings from the first few months at the Writers' Group:

> In conclusion, all life is an illusion. (September 19, 1996)

> Therefore, the entire upper world is nothing more than imaginary illusion. (September 26, 1996)

> However, after every reflection I still believe: Life is an illusion! (October 10, 1996)

These statements are not exceptions; he literally concluded everything he said or wrote during the first few months of attending the Writers' Group with a statement that life is only an illusion. What is interesting is how the group accepted him. Even if he wasn't really there, as he believed, he was still welcome to be there. One day he said that what he wrote was not very good, and I responded that it did not matter because neither he nor the writing existed, and he laughed. Slowly he started to integrate others' ideas and responses into his world. The change was gradual, often infinitesimal in degree, but still there, nonetheless.

Slowly, Warren started to transform, and began to take a more active interest in the outside world. This slow shift was revealed in his weekly writing. At the conclusion of a story entitled "Me and My Last Two Days of Frightening Non-Existence" Warren wrote:

> Now tonight, I have to talk to a sergeant at the morality squad. One slanderous statement on my part and I may be jailed. Then I may exist! (October 17, 1996)

Warren even jokes about his obsession about life being an illusion and his state of non-being. He also addresses the issue of having to speak with the police, a social connection that he could not ignore because of the law. At another writing session, one of the topics was about prejudice and racism. Warren concluded his short essay with the following sentence:

> In this essay, I have made no mention of non-existence and illusion. This is because a complex issue like prejudice rises above all abstract and non-existent beings. (October 24, 1996)

Warren felt that racism, as a social issue, was more important than his weekly debate about existence; in other words, he was engaged with the world. Warren's change in perception and attitude did not occur as a straightforward, linear progression. It was a recursive struggle, with Warren immersed in the tension of existence and nonexistence. For instance, for the next few weeks he concluded writings with the following lines:

> *And in the end I still have the conclusion*
> *That life is an illusion.* (November 7, 1996)

> *But most of all, in conclusion*
> *The life of man is one big illusion.* (November 7, 1996)

The struggle continued, as did the writing. Warren never missed a writing session, and continued to be actively involved in the Writers' Group. In the last paragraph of a piece of writing entitled "Abstract Art," Warren wrote:

> The waving green lines remind me of the absence of man himself from this earth. The orange colour reminds me of man's imagination which I use as proof of the non-existence of every single so-called physical and mental entity that there is. Everything in the solar system only exists in our imagination. And because our imagination doesn't exist, I take this as proof that there is no existing living or dead, organic or inorganic particle in this entire emptiness which man calls life! (November 14, 1996)

Warren's writing shows the intense inner struggle he was going through on a daily basis at that time in his life. The writing, though on the surface extremely bleak, is actually quite hopeful. Instead of merely saying that he did not exist and not writing anything more, he used an abstract painting hanging in the CMHA Board Room as a starting point to explore his own existence, much like one would use a Rorschach test.

Two weeks later, Warren wrote the following untitled piece during our writing session:

> During the past two weeks as I reflected at last's writer's group, there have been changes in my life and they are still coming.
>
> As I walked out of my apartment block tonight, I saw a shimmering spray of snow coming down. I then began walking to the street. The snow had such a brilliant white colour that I had noticed in the last decade or two. I looked up at the sky and saw the crisp clear blackness of the night. The blackness had a mix of white colour radiating from the white snow below. I had never noticed the moon have such a white crimson colour in about twenty years.
>
> As I looked skyward, I thought of things like God and love and the universe, from a way that I had never thought since I was a teenager.
>
> I could actually see the wonders of the stars. I thought, "Did everything happen by accident or was there a master creator?" At the present time, I simply do not know the answer, but then, does anyone?
>
> I will continue pondering the mysteries of life in my new vision. Perhaps someday I will satisfy my mind. (November 28, 1996)

During the same writing session as the above, Warren wrote a long essay called "Reflections on My Life" in which he mentioned a conversation with his doctor, and what he noticed about his life after the visit. In one paragraph he writes:

> In the last week I have continued to see the world in a new brilliance. For the first time in a decade, I feel as if I am a part of the world. (November 28, 1996)

He concludes the essay with the following paragraph:

> I realize that my health still has a long way to go before I will be well. But my doctor believes that my health will keep on improving. And I believe that some day my health will be good. And if you believe strong enough whether it's God or fate, anything is possible. (November 28, 1996)

Most of the writing Warren completed during these months at the Writers' Group would be considered to be in the expressive function. Often he would write about the past and memories; however because of the nature of the Writers' Group, he also had the opportunity to write about the suggested topics. During the next few weeks, he wrote about a variety of topics as is suggested by the following titles: "Autumn Leaves," "Buffalo Return to the Plains," "CPR Rail Life," "The Great Depression," "Mr. Manning," "Akhmantova" [sic, film title], "Politics," "Time" and "Today." Butler and Bentley (1997) would consider much of this writing as lifewriting with the writer engaged in writing as a means to make sense of life experience. There is an element of social and cultural connection; the titles suggest that Warren is also writing about topics that go beyond the self. Warren was now engaged actively in writing that explored social situations and issues. He had moved past the self-expressive mode to writing that engaged in a more social discussion. The following essay shows a further movement into an engagement with others and the world:

All My Yesterdays

> In the past I did not exist. Life was simply one big illusion. Nothing was real, not the earth, stars or God. The world was empty and lacked lustre. It did not sparkle with echoes of laughter. There was no fun in my adolescent years. The fun in my life had waxed and waned throughout my history.
>
> The last two months I have noticed a change. I can see some beauty in the world again. The stars sparkle with colour and the sun glistens with an angelic glow. This past Christmas was the best I had in about ten years. At the Christmas supper table, my family sat. There was turkey and all the Christmas food trimmings. The best part of Christmas this year was the saying of grace by my mother. She seemed to beam with such a beautiful radiance. The words seemed to remind me of my youth when I was happy. All I ask is that my tomorrows are happier than my yesterday. (January 30, 1997)

I want to reiterate that the changes Warren made were not in a direct, linear progression. Instead he used his writing to negotiate a sense of self, and that this site of negotiation was usually in a constant tension. For instance, a few weeks later, he wrote about his place in the world:

My Place in the Universe

> My place is on a tiny dot of something in the vast trillions of light years of the emptiness of space. I feel more as if I am a non-existent collection of atoms than an organized, god-like aggregate of human body parts. There is no absolute physical truth in me existing. There is only absolute philosophical truth. No concise factual proof but only a feeling. (February 6, 1997)

The following piece of writing clearly shows the emotional and psychological tension he was constantly experiencing at this time in his life:

My Life

> At the present time I am in a state of transition with no goal in sight. I simply live from day to day with no real idea of what's going to happen to me. I am enjoying life much more now than a year ago before I became involved with CMHA. I have some friends now as compared to zero friends a year ago. I am getting out of my apartment as compared to virtual isolation a year ago. I am happier and less depressed than a year ago. My thoughts are more organized now than a year ago. I am not as paranoid or suspicious of people as I was a year ago. But still there is a vacuum in my life. Is it caused by the lack of a firm belief in the supernatural or God? I have done a lot of thinking about God that last while. My heart and inner feelings tell me there is a God. But my mind and external feelings tell me there is not. Philosophically I have been led to believe there is no God. Morally and in real life I have been taught to believe in God. I realize no one has ever seen God but then I realize no one has ever seen atoms and yet we know they exist. I often think about what will happen to me in the future. When I do this my future seems bleak. When I look at the past, the past looks bleak. Right now I am only living in the present. I never have any idea what tomorrow may bring. My life truly has been one big tragedy. (March, 1996)

Warren uses his own writing to discover what is meaningful in his life. At the Writers' Group, Warren feels accepted and validated, and that no one judges him. Warren is therefore willing to take the risk to explore personal meaning in his writing. Using the expressive function of writing, he writes for himself, but also to be heard by other people. In the writing he constantly negotiates his place or position in the world among other people.

I will close with a longer piece of writing that was completed a few years after he had begun attending the Writers' Group. The content of the writing shows a deep connection with what Warren experienced at Writers' Group and the value he places on the writing he has completed.

Writer's Group: Learning

Ever since I started attending the writer's group a little over five years ago I have found the association of people a very cohesive and close-knit group of individuals. Each member has their own distinctive flavor of creative expression. The members have changed since I started coming. There have been writings on poems, editorials, journal articles, humor stories, personal life experiences, and almost every other imaginable form of writing. For me this group has been a positive bonus for my life. After nine years of sitting in isolation, the writer's group was where I had the pleasure of expressing my inner thoughts, hidden fears, and splendid moments of artistic freedom. The first summer in the group can be coined "the summer of regaining my life" or "freedom of '96."

Since that first summer things have changed some in my life. I have seen improvements in my health along with bad periods. But truly life is more pleasurable now than when I was by myself. To all the members of the writer's group and a special thank you to my mentors Sam and Jeff I truly owe a debt of gratitude. I salute each and every one of you.

(November 14, 2000)

Warren uses expressive writing as a zone of construction to conceptualize a sense of who he is in relation to others and the world. At the Writers' Group, Warren actively wrote and shared the writing by reading it aloud and discussing it. The acceptance of the group reduced Warren's fear and allowed him to explore his self as a series of relationships: to himself, to others, and to the world. For Warren, the act of writing and seeing the physical text of his words in a published form, affirmed his presence. By attending the Writers' Group, and actively using writing as a place to play, and discover, and explore, Warren wrote himself back into existence.

Chapter Seven

Revisiting Writing Process Theory

In this chapter, I revisit writing theory beginning with a reconceptualization of what it means to write in the expressive function (Britton, 1970; Britton et al., 1975) to include a more complex understanding of self and its relationship with others and society. In light of the relational aspects of expressive writing, and the social aspects of writing, I then examine writing of text as the creation of an artifact whose meaning is always contextualized in cultural and social relationships.

Britton et al. (1975) defined expressive writing as "writing close to the self, carrying forward the informal presuppositions of informal talk and revealing as much about the writer as about his matter" (p. 141). Britton and his fellow researchers believed the expressive function was "the matrix from which differentiated forms of mature writing are developed" (p. 144), and that it was underutilized in education, constituting only five to six percent of their student writing samples (p. 141). It is extremely important to understand the deep significance of these statements.

The Expressive Function and the Self

Britton's simple definition of expressive writing as "writing close to the self" seems to be self-evident, until one starts to question it more thoroughly. For instance, what is the self, and what is writing that is close to the self? These questions are complex and need to be explored more thoroughly. Much of the recent criticism directed at expressive pedagogy (Bartholomae, 1995; Faigley, 1992; Minock, 1994) can be traced to frustration with the assumptions that expressivist theorists appear to make concerning issues of self, and writing that is close to the self.

Faigley (1992) observes, "Since the beginning of composition teaching in the late nineteenth century, college writing teachers have been heavily invested in the stability of the self and the attendant beliefs that writing can be a means of self-discovery and intellectual self-realization" (p. 15). Looking back with the gift of hindsight, one could probably determine that Britton was somewhat romantic in his vision of the self, and its potential liberation through language. Faigley (1992) notes that "proponents of expressionistic rhetoric hold out that the main goal of writing is to probe one's sense of selfhood and that it is possible to convey authentic selfhood through original language" (p. 17). Britton does not always seem to question the complex relationship of language and self, and that language might not "mirror" the self (Rorty, 1979).

Britton's definition of expressive writing as "writing using language close to the self" is problematic for a number of reasons.[1] Many writing process advocates do not completely explore the relationship of self and language, and often assume that by utilizing language that is close to the self, a writer can express the self, and this expression can then be judged by its honesty, authentic voice, and integrity. Many of these assumptions have been adapted into practice without question. Macrorie's (1976) statement is indicative of this belief: "All good writers speak in honest voices and tell the truth" (p. 5). This type of pedagogic endorsement is of the sort that social constructivists, critical theorists, poststructuralists, and postmodernists love to see because it is so easy to attack in poststructuralist and philosophical terms: What is good? What is an honest voice? What is truth? What is the relationship between voice and truth? The subtext of Macrorie's statement is that a reality exists "out there," that it can be expressed with an "honest voice," and in doing so this would enable a writer to tell the truth about that reality. Many writing process advocates would consider these questions ridiculous and have based so much of their pedagogy on "honesty," "truth," "authentic voice," "real writing," and "honest writing." Because so much current writing-process practice is a direct or indirect result of Britton's theoretical structure, it is exceedingly important to re-examine this structure.

The relationship between writing and self is not as clear-cut as most readers understand Britton's definition. First, does it presume a knowable, unified self

---

1. One must remember the context of Britton's work and how revolutionary it was in many respects. He was probably the first composition theorist to use the work of Vygotsky (1930/1978, 1934/1999) as a theoretical basis to investigate the movement of thought to speech, and "inner speech" to writing.

that can be expressed and then communicated? Second, does it suggest that the self exists in isolation, and can be expressed as an entity, independent of all social factors? Third, does it assume that a self has an essence that can be expressed through language? Fourth, does it suggest that language can and does represent the self? Faigley (1992), using the lens of postmodern theory, "questions the existence of a rational, coherent self and the ability of the self to have privileged insight into its own processes. Postmodern theory denies that the self has universal and transcendent qualities but instead renders our knowledge of self as always contingent and always partial" (p. 111).

Britton did not fully explore the concept of the self, probably because he thought it was self-evident that the self was a person's inner being, and language was an expression of self. It is this somewhat romantic vision of self and language and, more specifically, self and writing, which needs to be explored, and perhaps reconceptualized.

There are several alternative perspectives to that of a unified, essential self that could be effectively included in a discussion of expressive writing. McAdams (1996), in *The Stories We Live by: Personal Myths and the Making of the Self*, claims "identity is a life story" that "is a personal myth that an individual begins working on in late adolescence and young adulthood in order to provide his or her life with unity or purpose and in order to articulate a meaningful niche in the psychosocial world" (p. 5). Human beings construct a sense of self through story, which according to McAdams, "is a natural package for organizing many different kinds of information. Storytelling appears to be a fundamental way of expressing ourselves and our world to others" (p. 27). McAdams believes "simply writing or performing a story about oneself can prove to be an experience of healing and growth" (p. 32), which again can give us a new perspective on the value of expressive writing, and the link between writing and being. For many of the writers at the CMHA Writers' Group, the act of writing helps create a sense of identity. They negotiate a sense of self in the act of writing and in the social responses of the other participants.

Bruner's (1987) ideas on narrative are relevant in this examination of the value of writing for the Writers' Group participants. Bruner claims, "we seem to have no other way of describing 'lived time' save in the form of narrative" (p. 12). Bruner suggests "we become the autobiographical narratives by which we 'tell about' our lives. And given the cultural shaping...we also become variants of the culture's canonical forms" (p. 15). It is important that Bruner mentions the culture of the individual and its canonical forms. We are not isolated individuals; instead we are part of an exceedingly complex social network. Bruner has kept developing these ideas throughout his career. In *Acts of Meaning*, Bruner

(1990) explores how humans engage in meaning-making. One of his observations has great relevance for the interrelationship between individuals and meaning-making:

> The symbolic systems that individuals used in constructing meaning were systems that were already in place, already "there," deeply entrenched in culture and language. They constituted a very special kind of communal tool kit, whose tools, once used, made the user a reflection of the community. (p. 11)

In other words, any expression of self is not a completely isolated event because it is always done in the context of culture and language. Geertz (1973) maintains, "there is no such thing as human nature independent of culture" (p. 49). The self, therefore, is a complex dialogical relationship with society, and cannot be expressed in complete isolation.

Writing theorists have begun to reexamine the idea of self in the writing process. Newkirk (1997) and Minock (1994) both mention Kinneavy's (1971) classic work, *A Theory of Discourse*, because of his perspective on the self. Kinneavy, using the philosophical ideas of Sartre and Merleau-Ponty, as well as Cassirer's conception of man as the "symbolic animal", creates a very useful model of the self. Kinneavy believed that the "self must be represented in its three basic dimensions and in the signal of its expression. The three dimensions are Being-for-Itself, Being-for-Others, and Being-in-the-World. The signal for self-expression is style" (Kinneavy, 1971, p. 405). Kinneavy recognized that a "self" does not exist in complete isolation. Instead, for Kinneavy, a self is a series of relationships. He claimed:

> A person achieves personality and, therefore, true self-expression when he has an authentic Being-for-Itself with an honest recognition and repudiation of his past, a vision of his future projects, an acceptance of his Being-for-Others, and an unillusioned picture of his Being-in-the-World. All of this will give him a unique style in his verbal expression. (pp. 405-406)

By enlarging the concept of the individual self to include the relationship with others and the world, we can look at expressive writing as a far more complex function than originally thought. Minock (1994) says, "The self is thus a dynamic of relationships, socially *and* individually constructed, and it will present itself differently in different kinds of writing. Kinneavy's view of self allows us to look at expressive writing as a series of dialogues—with the self, or with others, and or with ideas" (p. 168). Writing for the self, using language close to the self, is a much more complex act than first articulated by some of the early theorists. A self is not isolated; instead, a self is part of a complex matrix of relationships.

Expressive Writing as the Performance of the Self

Thomas Newkirk (1997) has recently considered writing to be a presentation of self, rather than an expression or reflection of self. Drawing upon the performative theory of Goffman (1959), Newkirk suggests that "all forms of 'self-expression,' all of our ways of 'being personal' are forms of performance, in Goffman's terms, a 'presentation of self'" (Newkirk, 1997, p. 3). In this sense expressive writing does not express a unified self, but rather it is a performance of self. Newkirk claims that "the key feature of these presentations is their selectivity; every act of self-presentation involves the withholding of information that might undermine the idealized impression the performer wants to convey" (p. 3). Changing the view of writing from one of expression, to one of performance has deep social and cultural ramifications. If a writer is performing a sense of self, rather than expressing a self, then what changes with how one understands the writing process terms of "voice," "truth-telling," "authenticity" and "honest" writing? For instance, Newkirk notes that "according to Goffman (1959), the key element of a socially competent performance is the ability to maintain a situation definition consistent with that of the audience. In these cases 'honest' can cue a mutually agreed-upon type of performance" (p. 5). An authentic voice, therefore, could be construed as a voice that the reader believes to be authentic in its performance. Writing, from this perspective, becomes a social and cultural event that goes beyond a personal expression.

Expressive Writing as a Site of Construction of Self

Newkirk's ideas regarding expressive writing as a site of performance have great significance. He maintains that the writing becomes a performance for others. But what if expressive writing is not only a performance but an actual site of construction of self? Foucault (1997), in his study of "the arts of oneself" (p. 207), states that as "an element of self training, writing has, to use an expression that one finds in Plutarch, an ethopoietic function: it is an agent of the transformation of truth into ethos" (p. 209). Foucault mentions two types of ethopoietic writing: *hupomnemata* and *correspondence* (p. 209). *Hupomnemata*, which "could be an account book, public registers, or individual notebooks serving as memory aids" acted as "books of life, as guides for conduct" (p. 209). The writing of *hupomnemata* "provided a material and a framework for exercises to be carried out frequently: reading, rereading, meditating, conversing with oneself and with others...for a purpose that is nothing less than the shaping of the self" (pp. 210-211). The members of the Writers' Group engage in maintaining collections or notebooks of their writings, and their collected writings are published each year. For the participants of the Writers' Group, the act of writing engages the self, while also engaging others. Foucault states that *hupomnemata* enables "the formation of the self out of the collected discourse of others" (p. 217). In this sense, the act of writing "as a personal exercise done by and for oneself is an act of disparate truth" (p. 212). According to Foucault, *hupomnemata* "constituted a material record of things read, heard, or thought, thus offering them up as a kind of accumulated treasure for subsequent rereading and meditation" (p. 209). In this case, a writer is recording fragments of texts for the purpose of helping him understand and construct a sense of self. It is as if a writer, in picking up little pebbles from the stream of other discourses, discovers a sense of self in the process of making the language his or her own.

The second form of ethopoietic writing, *correspondence*, is "something more than a training of oneself by means of writing, through the advice and opinions one gives to the other: it also constitutes a certain way of manifesting oneself to oneself and to others" (Foucault, 1997, p. 216). Thus, for Foucault, *correspondence* is a complex means of constructing an identity within the "the reciprocity of the gaze and the examination" (p. 216) of the other. "The letter that, as an exercise, works toward the subjectivation of true discourse, its assimilation and its transformation as a 'personal asset,' also constitutes, at the same time, an objectification of the soul" (pp. 216-217). In other words, the writer makes the discourse his or her own, while at the same time objectifying his or her identity for others. This construction of self is most prevalent in what Britton has called expressive language. Instead of perceiving expressive writing as merely personal writing that uses language that is close to the self, it is perhaps preferable to see expressive writing as an extremely complex function in which the writer constructs the self and learns to project and even perform this self to others. Bakhtin's (1981, 1986, 1994) work with language, and the complex relationship with culture and society, is valuable at this point.

Bakhtin and Appropriation of Language

Bakhtin (1986, 1994) mentions that most individual language use is appropriated from the discourse of others. Bakhtin's term *heteroglossia* summarizes the complexity of the relationship between an individual and the culture to which she belongs: "every utterance contains within it the trace of other utterances, both in the past and in the future" (Bakhtin, 1994, p. 249). Bakhtin (1981) states that the "authentic environment of an utterance, the environment in which it lives and takes shape, is dialogized heteroglossia, anonymous and social as language, but simultaneously concrete, filled with specific intent and accented as an individual utterance" (p. 272). In this sense, expressive writing can be seen in all its complexity: the writer, working within the discourses of others, makes the language his or her own and in doing so communicates a sense of self to both oneself and others. Meaning is created in the matrix of relationships, both social and linguistic. Bakhtin (1981) states:

> As a living, socio-ideological concrete thing, as hetroglot opinion, language, for the individual consciousness, lies on the borderline between oneself and the other. The word in language is half someone else's. It becomes "one's own" only when the speaker populates it with his own intention, his own accent, when he appropriates the word, adapting it to his own semantic and expressive intention. Prior to this moment of appropriation, the word does not exist in a neutral and impersonal language (it is not, after all, out of a dictionary that the speaker gets his words!), but rather it exists in other people's mouths, in other people's contexts, serving other people's intentions: it is from there that one must take the word, and make it one's own. (pp. 293-294)

In making language her own, an individual also creates or constructs a self that can then be objectified through text, and presented to others (Foucault, 1997). Writing in this sense can be seen as a technology that changes an individual's consciousness and sense of self (Ong, 1982). Ong states:

> Without writing, the literate mind would not and could not think as it does, not only when engaged in writing but normally even when it is composing its thoughts in oral form. More than any other single invention, writing has transformed the human consciousness. (p. 78)

An individual's consciousness is altered through the act of writing. It is within the expressive function that the appropriation of language (Bakhtin, 1986, 1994) and the "shaping of self" (Foucault, 1988, 1997) take place. Expressive writing acts as the matrix for the other writing functions for reasons that were far more complex than Britton may have assumed. Because of the complexity of the social relationships and language appropriation that takes place in expressive writing, the social aspects of writing need to be reexamined.

A Site of Multi-Perspectives: Social Complexity and the Self

The social aspects of the Writers' Group are extremely complex and significant, and go far beyond the level of entertainment or enjoyment. At the Writers' Group, the participants enjoy each other's company, feel accepted for who they are as people, and are allowed to "just be." Yet it is important to remember that the central activity of the Writers' Group is not visiting or joking or talking. It is the act of writing.

Although there are other social activities at the CMHA, the Writers' Group is by far the most successful, and the one with the most longevity. The reasons for this success are actually quite complex. The act of writing, and the intense work involved with writing, is one of the most important attractions of the group for many participants. At the Writers' Group, the participants are taken seriously as writers, as well as people. They have a place where they connect with other people, and where they can discuss and debate ideas and concepts. The Writers' Group provides a lively, stimulating, and often exciting environment that is safe and secure. The writers are exposed to different ideas and different perspectives. Yet the value of the Writers' Group goes beyond the social aspect because it is also a place where work is conceptualized and completed. The writing is always the focus of the group.

As Elbow (2000) suggested in his reexamination of freewriting, there is a social element to the writing, resulting in a sharing of space, as well as a sharing of activity. I would add that at the Writers' Group, the sharing of the created texts is equally important. The texts exist as artifacts that can be explored from cultural, social and individual bases from both the writers' and the readers' points of view. Although it is true that the writers exist in a social environment, it is equally true that the writing as text also exists in a social and cultural relationship. The writing acts as a site of exploration of self and the culture that one exists within. For the participants of the Writers' Group it is important to share the writing with others. In doing so, the writing allows the writers to examine the matrix of relationships within themselves, as Kinneavy (1971) has suggested through his concept of a self as Being-for-Itself, Being-for-Others, and Being-in-the-World. Finally, the social aspect of the Writers' Group allows the writers to share these explorations with others by reading the writings as text to the other members, and providing feedback to one another.

Text as Cultural Artifact

The writing as text has great importance to the writers, and the content always has significance. After the writers read their work, there is always a brief discussion and acknowledgment of the content. This does not mean the others agree or that they reach consensus on the writer's ideas, however, there is acceptance of the ideas, and validation of those ideas even if they are disagreed with. In other words, the writers at CMHA are taken seriously as writers. One reason is the attention and respect mutually given to their writing as product. This seriousness is carried over into the publication of the yearly book, which as I have mentioned earlier, all the writers look forward to each year. Blake (1995) suggests that:

> Emphasis in the process-writing classroom has typically and traditionally been placed on the process by which students create texts...it is just as crucial to emphasize the product, or the cultural text which they produce...an emphasis needs to be placed on

> not only how the text is socially and culturally constructed from such notions as gender, race, and class but on what the text actually says, revealing issues of gender, race, and class. (p. 175)

In this sense, writing as text becomes a site of meaning-making both within the writer—always considering the matrix of relationships that are constantly negotiated (Being-for-Itself, Being-for-Others, Being-in-the-World)—and beyond the writer as a site of negotiation between writer and reader. The writing as text considered as a cultural artifact becomes a site of meaning-making for both the writer and the reader. Blake (1995) writes that because "all language is social, writing becomes a social activity in which a community of writers interacts to negotiate and construct meaning and texts" (p. 166). At the CMHA Writers' Group, the negotiation and construction of texts and meanings is the central activity of the weekly sessions for the writers. The reading aloud of the texts, and the sharing with the rest of the group, is of prime importance to them.

Lensmire (1994a, 1994b, 1997, 1998, 2000) has been critical of writing-process and writing-workshop advocates because of a romantic bias that often ignores the complex cultural and social issues that are reflected in the products, or texts, of the writing. He maintains that instructors often ignore the issues of race, gender, and social inequality in their teaching of writing. At the Writers' Group, these issues are never ignored; rather they are embraced. Through writing, and the resulting discussions, the participants explore ideas in a social situation of acceptance, though individuals often hold opposing viewpoints. Lensmire (1994b, 2000) has suggested using Bakhtin's (1984) notion of carnival as a metaphor to understand writing groups. Lensmire (1994b) emphasizes four features of carnival life, and believes that the first three features, "active participation, free and familiar contact among people, and a playful, familiar relation to the world" are "prominent and positive features of the writing workshops" as practiced by most advocates (Atwell, 1987; Calkins, 1986, 1991; Graves, 1983; Murray, 1985). These features of writing workshop "grant students control (or 'ownership') over their own literate activities...which helps them regain their interest in and commitment to expressing themselves in print" (Lensmire, 1994b, p. 376). Lensmire, however, notes that one of the most important of the carnival laws "is the seeming obliteration of the official, established order" (p. 374), and he suggests that what is missing from writing- group practice is the fourth feature of carnival life, "what Bakhtin calls carnival abuse, or profanation" (p. 375). Profanation, according to Bakhtin, is "both negative and positive, both destructive and regenerating" (Lensmire, 1994b, p. 375). Profanation allows the participants to see life in all its complexity because in carnival "people laughed at ideas and practices supposed to be universal and eternal and saw them for what they were—partial and contingent" (p. 375). The CMHA Writers' Group allows for profanation—everything is questioned and nothing is taken for granted. The group practices what I would call an irreverent respect for each other and me. Because attendance at the writing sessions is completely voluntary and based only on personal interest, issues of authority are often turned upside down. If the attendees do not like what is going on, they can simply leave or not attend. This awareness leads to a freedom that is seldom seen in school practice. Writers at the Writers' Group can, and do, address any issue they want, thus creating the "critical, radical edge of Bakhtin's carnival" (Lensmire, 1994b, p. 380) that Lensmire believes is missing from most writing workshops. The writing that occurs at the CHMA Writers' Group is not isolated from social and cultural issues, and is never a manifestation of "dummy runs" (Britton et al., 1975, p. 104). The writing is real and valuable to all the members and represents an empowerment that deeply affects their lives.

Writing always has a bidirectional movement, both inner and outer, and contains both personal and social elements. The act of writing has an inner movement, which results in nothing less than the construction of self, as well as an outer movement, because the writing as text exists as a cultural artifact that is meant for others to read. It is extremely important to acknowledge the significance of both movements, and the complexity of what it means to write and the value writing has for the writer.

Expressive Writing as Matrix

Britton (1979) suggested that expressive writing formed the matrix from which all other forms of writing develop. He states:

> We set up a developmental hypothesis, the hypothesis that expressive writing should be regarded as a matrix from which the other two categories would develop. That is to say, expressive writing might be seen as a beginner's all purpose instrument; and "learning to write" would involve the progressive evolution both of the other two forms, transactional and poetic, and of the mature forms of expressive writing that we continue to use in personal letters and the like. (p. 124)

Britton's ideas on expressive writing are profound, though not without problems. He never clarifies how the writing evolves or moves from the expressive function to the poetic and transactional functions. He also suggests that writing in the expressive function should develop to more mature forms of expressive writing without specifying what those forms are.

Minock (1994) critiques Britton's hypothesis but changes his wording slightly, by stating that his hypothesis "posits that expressive writing leads naturally and inevitably to other forms of writing" (p. 154). She also claims that Britton "believes that expressive writing leads progressively to academic writing" (p. 155). Her summation of Britton's ideas and her wording regarding the movement of expressive writing ("gradually grow"; "leads naturally and inevitably"; "leads progressively" [p. 154-155]) is somewhat inaccurate. Britton carefully uses more subtle verbs, such as "move" and "evolve," to denote the shift to other forms of writing from the expressive function, rather than verbs that denote a natural or inevitable growth. Expressive writing is not the compost heap from which all other forms of writing naturally grow. Instead the shift from personal writing to the poetic and transactional functions needs to address different discourses and genre structures, as well as the variety of intended audience. Her critique, however, does accurately address how writing-process and writing-group advocates have adopted many of Britton's ideas. Britton did not adequately address how one writing function moves to another, though he did provide some insight into his thinking. Regarding the move from the expressive function, he writes:

> Thus it may be that, as a writer moves from the expressive into the transactional, he increasingly takes over responsibility for rules of use that, in sum total, constitute one kind of order, one mode or organization by which we encode experience. (Britton et al., 1975, p. 85)

and

> The development from the expressive to poetic is associated, in our view, with a learning process, but one of a different kind (perhaps one that is not often thought of as "learning"). (Britton, 1979, p. 127)

In both cases, Britton appears to be suggesting that the movement, by depending on either a learning process, or taking over more responsibility for the rules of use, must address the issue of language structure, and the "mode or organization by which we encode experience" (Britton et al., 1975, p. 85). Therefore, the movement from the expressive is not one of natural growth; instead the movement must be deliberate and must include an awareness of structure and audience.

Bartholomae (1995) and Elbow (1995) have engaged in an interesting debate concerning the use of personal writing in academic settings, with Elbow arguing for the utilization of personal writing and Bartholomae maintaining that academic discourse needs to be the focus for student writers. Both positions have merit, but what is ultimately needed is for the writer to make the discourse part of his or her own language use in a meaningful way. If a student simply adopts the academic discourse without understanding or without making the language one's own, the resulting writing will either be meaningless, sterile or a form of plagiarism, which could be construed as an appropriation without individual meaning-making.

Macrorie (1988) called this type of meaningless writing, "Engfish...the say-nothing, feel nothing, word wasting pretentious language of the schools" (p. 22). Macrorie's solution was the I-Search paper, which he described as:

> not Re-Searches, in which the job is to search again what someone has already searched—but original searches in which persons scratch an itch they feel...to fulfil a need, not that the teacher has imagined for them, but one they feel themselves. (p. 14)

Macrorie's I-Search concept combines academic rigor and documentation with an individual's motivation and drive. In other words, the expressive function is being moved into the transactional function in a meaningful way, while at the same time making the students aware of academic discourse.

Similar moves to the transactional and poetic functions can be encouraged by providing students with meaningful reasons to learn different writing structures, and engage actively in different and meaningful discourse communities. Genre theorists (Cope & Kalantzis, 1993; Cranny-Francis & Martin, 1993; Freedman & Medway, 1994a, 1994b; Painter & Martin, 1985; Swales, 1990) have suggested that genre structures have great importance. Genre theorists "acknowledge some kind of dialectical reflexivity between text and context, between genre and culture, between writing and subjectivity" (Freedman & Medway, 1994a, p. ix). It is possible that writing in the expressive function can move to poetic and transactional functions with a meaningful engagement with other discourse communities and genres.

In a discussion with me concerning the value of personal writing, and the difficulty some beginning writers have in creating short stories, the Canadian writer Guy Vanderhaeghe (1982, 1996, 2002) maintained:

> Anytime you move from personal writing, or what you call expressive writing, to an academic or even personal essay, or a work of fiction, there has to be an awareness, on some level, of structure and form. You can't write a short story, for instance, without some knowledge of how a short story is put together. (personal communication, August 14, 2001)

Perhaps what is needed in the teaching of writing is a deeper awareness of how language functions in a social sense. The structures and forms that Vanderhaeghe mentions are social agreements in many ways. The academic writing Bartholomae (1995) argues for is simply another form of discourse that students need to be exposed to in order that they can make it their own. This engagement needs to be meaningful, and will not "naturally grow" from expressive writing; however, it is equally important to acknowledge that academic writing cannot have significance or meaning if the writer does not make it his or her own. In his study of expressive writing and academic writing, Allen (2000) writes:

> How does the making of stories in this blend of the academic and the personal stimulate development? The answer cannot be easy because the elements—self, expression, development—are complex and elusive. I suggest that the results I report here arise from three kinds of relatedness encouraged, or permitted, by the process I have described: the relation of the self to meaning, the relation of self to the self, and the relation of self to language. (p. 280)

Allen acknowledges the complex relationship between self and language. This relationship is crucial to an understanding of the true value of writing to individuals because writing is both a technology for communication, and a technology for the construction of the self. The technologies work in conjunction with one other. The writing has both an inner movement and an outer movement.\

All meaningful writing engages the self and others and the world in a complex, dialogical relationship—meaning is always contextual. The self constantly constructs itself and negotiates meaning with others in a series of social agreements. Bruner (1990) in *Acts of Meaning* writes about the complex relationship between self and culture:

> The Self, then, like any other aspect of human nature, stands both as a guardian of permanence and as a barometer responding to the local cultural weather. The culture, as well, provides us with guides and stratagems for finding a niche between stability and change: it exhorts, forbids, lures, denies, rewards the commitments that the Self undertakes. And the Self, using its capacities for reflection and for envisaging alternatives, escapes or embraces or reevaluates and reformulates what the culture has on offer. Any effort to understand the nature and origins of Self is, then, an interpretive effort akin to that used by a historian or an anthropologist trying to understand a "period" or a "people." And ironically enough, once an official history or anthropology has been proclaimed in a culture and enters the public domain, that very fact alters the process of Self-construction. (p. 110)

A writer, in creating a text, negotiates a meaningful relationship between a self and a culture, with the text acting as the interface. To borrow a biological and ecological term, meaning and communication are created in the space between self and others in the metaphorical space of the riparian zone.

Expressive Writing as a Riparian Zone

In ecological terminology, a riparian zone is the forested land along rivers, streams, and lakes, and forms the transition area between upland and aquatic ecosystems. I have chosen the metaphor of the riparian zone for a number of reasons. The word riparian comes from the Latin word "ripa," meaning riverbank, which can also be seen as an edge. Riparian zones are among the most diverse biological systems in the world, although they comprise a very small proportion of landmass. Riparian zones act as filtering systems for water, and provide shelter and travel routes for wildlife. Riparian zones are therefore sites of nourishment, shelter and safety in movement for animals. I suggest that we think of expressive writing as a place where self and culture meet—a place that is both a zone of construction of the self, and a site of negotiation of meaning between the personal and the social. In writing in the expressive function, writers are in the riparian zone, traveling and finding nourishment as well as refuge and safety. Yet the riparian zone also represents the edge of self, that point of contact with the rest of the world and others.

Thinking of the meeting of self and culture as a riparian zone can help educators consider the complexity of this encounter. For example, the meeting of personal literacies and academic discourses can be conceived as a riparian zone with a diverse living component. Writing within the academic discourse with no acknowledgment of self and contextualized meaning leads to *Engfish* (Macrorie, 1988). Yet writing that only stays on the level of the strictly personal becomes solipsism. It is within the riparian zone, where self meets culture and others, that a writer constructs true meaning. A writer writes both the self and the culture, and, in the process of doing so, changes both. There is a mutuality, or bi-directional movement, implied in the act of writing that impacts at the tension point of contact within the metaphoric space of the riparian zone.

Expressive Writing as School Practice

The expressive function is an underutilized form of writing in most school systems (Britton et al., 1975, p. 141). The use of expressive writing could validate the individual within the school system and society, both of which are often perceived as monolithic structures by students. Expressive writing is a central technology in negotiating meaning and identity in the matrix of relationships—both the self as an inner relationship, including Being-for-Itself, Being-for-Others and Being-in-the-World (Kinneavy, 1971, pp. 405-406), and the self in relationship with culture and the larger society.

Many curriculum and educational documents are being rewritten to reflect a more profound awareness of diversity. Expressive writing has great potential as a tool to negotiate this interaction with others to come to a clearer understanding of the complexity of the personal, social, and cultural aspects of school learning. This type of writing practice in education is in keeping with Freire's

(1994, 1995; Freire & Macedo, 1987) vision of meaningful education with the acknowledgment of a "unity in diversity" and a "oneness in difference" (1994, p. 151). Freire (1995) maintains that:

> People, as beings "in a situation," find themselves rooted in temporal-spatial conditions which mark them and which they also mark. They will tend to reflect on their own "situationality" to the extent that they are challenged by it to act upon it. Human beings *are* because they *are* in a situation. And they *will be more* the more they not only critically reflect upon their existence but critically act upon it. (p. 90)

Encouraging the use of expressive writing in school practice would create the metaphoric space of the riparian zone, in which writers and teachers could negotiate meanings and relationships for students as individuals. As Freire (1985) says, "reading words, and writing them, must come from the dynamic movement of reading the world" (p. 19). This would signal a dramatic shift in educational practice: students would be encouraged to actively engage in the world and culture, and educators would be encouraged to actually validate the students they teach as valuable individuals. Expressive writing could function as the site of meaning-negotiation for a better understanding of self in relation to others and the world. For Freire "education is simultaneously an act of knowing, a political act, and an artistic event" (p. 17). This subtle shift is also in keeping with recent change in school practice, moving from a transmission model of instruction to one of transactional, or even transformational instruction, based on a social constructivist perspective of learning (Miller & Seller, 1985). Writing in the expressive function lends itself to this type of meaning making.

bell hooks (1999) mentions writing in a diary as a child, an acceptable act in her family because "it was writing that was never meant to be read by anyone" (p. 4). For hooks, however, this type of writing was "the space for critical reflection where I struggled to understand myself and the world around me, that crazy world of family and community, that painful world" (p. 5). hooks mentions that this type of writing "has most assuredly been a writing act that intimately connects the art of expressing one's feelings on the written page with the construction of self and identity with the effort to be fully self-actualized" (p. 5). hooks describes an act of actively constructing a sense of self, as well as negotiating meaning with the culture she lives within. For hooks, "writing was the healing place where I could collect the bits and pieces, where I could put them together again" (p.7) because, as she notes, "written words change us all and make us more than we could ever be without them" (p. xvi).

Shafer (2001), in his work with a community of female prisoners, echoes hooks' ideas when he writes: "In their world, writing transcends the scholarly and pragmatic concerns of the typical student and often becomes a kind of instrument of exploration" (p. 75). Shafer used personal writing in his workshops that gave:

> students the opportunity to voice their latent feelings about incarceration and the life they were living. This was their opportunity to articulate their emerging understanding of who they were. The writing class would be a venue for personal reflection that would provide a voice for their pasts and futures. It would, it seemed, give meaning to their lives. (p. 76)

In doing so Shafer allowed the women to actively engage the world and "to use language to solve problems and understand their world" (p. 76). Shafer refers to Giroux's (1997) contention that pedagogy should strive to empower each student with an "active critical consciousness" (Shafer, 2001, p. 76). Expressive writing, in its engagement with self, can also be a central tool in negotiating meaning with society and culture. Seen in this way, "writing introduces division and alienation, but a higher unity as well. It intensifies the sense of self and fosters more conscious interaction between persons. Writing is consciousness-raising" (Ong, 1982, p. 179). Expressive writing is the zone of construction of the self, as well as the site of negotiation for meaning between the self and the culture. Educators have tended to underestimate the value and power of expressive writing. If we are serious about true transformational learning, then we need to delve deeply into the complex relationship between self and language, or "what Foucault would see as the archaeological conversation producing selves and cultures" (White & Hellerich, 1998, p. 2). The self writes the culture and the culture writes the self. Expressive writing, therefore, has a bi-directional movement: writing acts inward to help construct a sense of identity; and the writing also acts as a cultural artifact that writes the culture.

In emphasizing the process ,writing process advocates have sometimes underestimated the value of the product. As Foucault (1997) notes in his discussion of correspondence, the writer reads what he writes. This has great consequence because:

> The new care of the self involved a new experience of self....A relation developed between writing and vigilance. Attention was paid to nuances of life, mood, and reading, and the experience of self was intensified and widened by virtue of this act of writing. A whole field of experience opened which earlier was absent. (pp. 232–233)

Writing in the expressive function is a far more complex act than has been validated in most educational practices. The self and the culture are in relationship. Yet how does one access this relationship in writing practice in a meaningful way?

Freewriting at the Writers' Group

In the ten years that I've been involved with the Writers' Group, we have written on hundreds of topics using numerous genres. Coming from a background of teaching writing, I utilized writing-process theory, as well as pedagogical practices of writing workshop. I used a number of heuristics, including outlining, idea maps, clustering, freewriting, brainstorming and poetic forms to motivate the group writing. I had all the writers at various times use a sequence of writing activities that could be said to follow a simple five-step process model of prewriting, writing, revising, editing and publishing. The results were very, very successful, with the exception of revision. When I first introduced the idea of revision, or what Murray (1999) calls "re-vision" (p. 202), the writers at CMHA would often simply write a new piece on a similar topic, or often a new piece on a brand-new topic. There are several possible explanations. Either I was not teaching the process correctly, or the writers lacked some skill or technique or ability, or the process theory was lacking in some understanding of what goes on when a writer writes. After pondering this issue for several years, I suggest that what occurs at the Writers' Group might be helpful in a considering what it means to write, and how writers actually go about writing.

Much of the writing that occurs at the CMHA Writers' Group could be classified as freewriting. The group loves to write on a topic "off the top of their heads." They inevitably find this activity exciting, and I've always been surprised by what they create in the ten to fifteen minutes we usually write. The writers keep coming back to this activity, thoroughly engaged in what Elbow (1973/1998) calls the "believing game" which he sees as "the dialectic of experience because the more you get ideas and perceptions into the most fully experienced form, the better it works" (p. 171). The writers are engrossed in what they do, suggesting a complete surrender to the activity of writing. Nachmanovitch (1990) suggests that "to create, we need both technique and freedom from technique" (p. 73). The CMHA writers engage in freewriting so completely the writing almost becomes unconscious. Nachmanovitch in discussing the idea of play writes:

> To this end we practice until our skills become unconscious. If you had to think consciously about the steps involved in riding a bicycle, you'd fall off at once. Part of the alchemy engendered by practice is a kind of cross-trading between conscious and unconscious. Technical how-to-information of a deliberate and rational kind drops through long repetition from consciousness so that we can "do it in our sleep." (pp. 73-74)

It is possible that the writers are able to use technique in writing without thinking about it on a cognitive level. Caroline, in describing how she wrote her novel, says, "It wasn't a thought process. It was just writing." In other words, Caroline was so engaged in the act of writing, she no longer had to think about it, an experience similar to what Csikszentmihalyi (1997b) calls flow, "an almost automatic, effortless, yet highly focused state of consciousness" (p. 110). Csikszentmihalyi notes that when an individual is deeply involved in some activities like music or sports, it often "becomes autotelic, which is Greek for something that is an end in itself" (p. 110). He notes that "most things in life are exotelic" (p. 110), which are done to attain an external goal. Csikszentmihalyi maintains that "the secret to a happy life is to learn to get flow from as many of the things we have to do as possible. If work and family life become autotelic, then there is nothing wasted in life, and everything we do is worth doing for its own sake" (pp. 111-112). At the Writers' Group, the participants engage in writing for writing's sake, as an autotelic activity, which is both pleasurable and self-empowering.

I do not want to suggest that editing, or revising or completing drafts are not important. For instance, Elbow (1973/1998) suggests that these are important activities for the "doubting game" which he sees as "gaining a monopoly on legitimacy in our culture" (p. 150). I am only suggesting that we need to put more faith in the creation and conceptualization of ideas and thoughts before we immediately start to criticize, or edit them. Freewriting holds some interesting possibilities. What is needed is to reconceptualize what is involved in the act of freewriting, and to look at the value this type of writing holds for many writers. Elbow (2000) notes that when "my writing goes well, it is usually because the plan itself—my sense of where I'm trying to get my material to go—came to me in a piece of noncontrolled writing. Freewriting doesn't just give 'content,' it also gives 'form'," (pp. 132-133). Elbow also suggests that "freewriting is an invitation to stop writing and instead to 'be written'" (p. 131). It is possible that freewriting in the expressive function is the best means to enter the riparian zone that exists between self and culture.

Freewriting and Freewrighting

One means of changing the perspective on freewriting is a simple shift in perspective to view it as the creation, or performance, of a legitimate piece of writing, instead of an heuristic or practice that leads to a piece of writing. Freewriting should be seen both as performance and as practice. Once the writing exists as text, as an object or an artifact, it can then be manipulated and molded and changed. I suggest that we reconsider freewriting, as freewrighting. Perhaps the neologism I am advocating may help conceptualize the shift in thinking. The semantic and linguistic shift from freewriting to freewrighting (using the word as one would for playwrighting, or millwrighting) focuses the central activity involved on the construction aspects of writing, rather than on the heuristic concerns of gathering or collecting ideas to be used later. This shift in the word accomplishes two things: one, it makes us aware that the writing as text is an artifact that is constructed with language; and two, that this language communicates, articulates, and expresses the thoughts, feelings and ideas of an individual who is part of a complex matrix of meaning involving others and the world.

Freewrighting can therefore be seen as both an exploration of the riparian zone between self and culture and also as the production of a cultural artifact that can then be manipulated and revised. Freewrighting provides a possible entry into all types of writing, though the first exploration is usually in the expressive function. With a knowledge of the writing text as a cultural artifact, the writing can then be moved into the poetic and transactional writing functions according to Britton's (1970, 1975) model. The writing as text needs to be seen as both a product of the self, and yet independent of the self. As Ong (1982) notes:

> Though inspiration derives from unconscious sources, the writer can subject the unconscious inspiration to far greater conscious control than the oral narrator. The writer finds his written words accessible for reconsideration, revision and other manipulations. (p. 148)

Writing always creates a text that is then objectified and removed from the self. Even if the text is about the self, as soon as a text is written it exists as an artifact or product. Ideas are always conveyed through language which is socially and culturally constructed. A writer both creates language and is created by language.

The Writer Writes the Self and Others

Jackson Pollock stated that "painting is a state of being….Painting is self-discovery. Every good painter paints what he is" (cited in Rodman, 1957, p. 82). Equally true is that every good writer writes what he is. Macrorie (1988) quotes the poet William Carlos Williams:

> A writer is a person whose best is released in the accomplishment of writing….He does not necessarily think these things—he does not, that is, think them out and then write them down: he writes, and the best of him, in spite even of his thought, will appear on the page even to his surprise, unrecognized or even sometimes against his will, by proper use of words. (p. 1)

Instead of conceiving writing as the process of organizing ideas and communicating them to others, in other words processing a product for delivery to others, we need to go beyond the limitations of the metaphor. We need to go beyond the manufacturing metaphor, to pay more attention to the value of a writer writing who he is. To do this, educators might reconsider the powerful value that writers ascribe to writing, especially writing that theorists would label as being in the expressive function.

Educators need to acknowledge at least two major considerations with the teaching of writing. They need to make students aware that the act of writing, no matter how personal, creates a text that exists as an artifact for others. In this way, students learn to create distance from the text, which will allow revision, or reworking of the text as artifact. Just as importantly, educators could recognize that student writing is connected to a sense of self, and is not easily objectified. Teachers teach students, not just the curriculum and the subject content, and they could validate students as individuals with unique perspectives and needs. As Kress (1997) has noted, educators work to define a "different task and status for individuals, one in which they have to be fully competent in the use of the resources of making meaning, but in which they are seen as creative, innovative, productive, acting out of their perceived needs" (p. 151). In this way, both educators and students learn that "literacy is best understood as a myriad of discursive forms and cultural forms and cultural competencies that construct and make available the various relations and experiences that exist between learners and the world" (Giroux, 1987, p. 10). Expressive writing becomes a central component of an education that allows for the construction of an individual's sense of self and negotiation with culture.

Bruner (1986) believes that humans have two modes or ways of knowing, the narrative and the paradigmatic. I would propose that in the expressive functions a writer creates meaning through narrative in a holistic manner, and not strictly through paradigmatic or linear, logico-rational thought. Narrative knowing, or storied knowing, always works in context and in relationship to others. Expressive writing as a place of discovery or exploration is where meaningful, narrative knowing can be created. Furthermore, the movement of writing from the expressive function to the transactional and poetic functions not only involves the knowledge of the genre structure, but also requires a shift in thinking from a narrative way of knowing to a paradigmatic way of knowing.

Expressive writing is far more complex than originally perceived by most researchers. Instead of being marginalized, expressive writing becomes the focus of true transformative education. In expressive writing, the two kinds of knowing, narrative and paradigmatic, are entwined, and meaning is created both for oneself and the culture. In the space of the riparian zone, meaning is created and transformation occurs. Through writing in the expressive function individuals construct a sense of self, and negotiate relationships with others and the world

Chapter Eight

Pedagogy of the Riparian Zone

What sets worlds in motion is the interplay of differences, their attractions and repulsions. Life is plurality, death is uniformity. By suppressing differences and peculiarities, by eliminating different civilizations and cultures, progress weakens life and favors death. The ideal of a single civilization for everyone, implicit in the cult of progress and technique, impoverishes and mutilates us. Every view of the world that becomes extinct, every culture that disappears, diminishes a possibility of life.

Octavio Paz,
The Labyrinth of Solitude

In moving from writing theory to pedagogy to praxis, educators are invited to consider the metaphorical spaces involved in the act of writing. In this final chapter, I explore and describe the pedagogical space that allows a writer to enter the riparian zone to explore the relationship between self and others, and to negotiate meaning in a contextual relationship within society and culture. A pedagogical shift in perspective is required to integrate and implement a riparian zone in writing groups, composition classes and most educational situations. What is constructed in any learning situation is a space within a space. The metaphor of the riparian zone is enfolded and nested within the larger pedagogical space.

There are no easy, prescriptive methodologies, nor step-by-step programs for the creation of this pedagogical space—although there are general principles that can be applied to most writing situations. These principles are scattered throughout the text and narratives of this book, but I will attempt to gather them in this chapter. For these principles to make sense, it is perhaps useful to consider a class or writing workshop as not simply a collection of people confined in a physical space defined by an architectural design, but rather as the complex matrix of relationships of the people within that space.

The Negotiation of Power

The teacher, first of all, has a responsibility to the group and herself to create a safe pedagogical space that allows the individual writer to enter the riparian zone with her own writing. To do this effectively, the teacher must be aware of the power relationships within the group, honestly acknowledge these issues of power, and remain conscious of them at all times. A teacher, educator or writing instructor invites the participants to enter a pedagogical space that is non-threatening, fruitful, hospitable, safe, playful, deeply generative, and contained within an atmosphere of trust and confidentiality.

In this model, the teacher is not simply an authoritative figure who instructs and controls the people within the space. Instead, the teacher is open to the paradox of being both in control and not in control, while maintaining a source of non-judgmental power that allows each member to have his or her own agency and identity. This role is not as difficult or complex as it may first appear, providing the teacher creates a space of trust, and is open to participating actively within that space while holding the same responsibilities as any other member. The teacher, operating from a non-authoritarian position of power, becomes a facilitator encouraging the expression of each writer's ideas. In this sense, the teacher operates from a level of power that is perceived as being equal to the students. All the participants are honored and respected as equals, and all have the right to voice their ideas. Yet at the same time the teacher holds a non-judgmental, yet authoritative, power that protects all members. The teacher has the responsibility to create a sense of trust and confidence within the membership so that group members eventually protect themselves and each other within that space. In this sense, the pedagogical space contains trust and becomes a community where sharing of ideas and thoughts is allowed and encouraged without the threat of dominance. Constant vigilance is required, and the teacher uses danger points constructively as teaching moments, which are not denied or avoided. The teacher is therefore required to engage fully and listen deeply to others, while encouraging reciprocity at all times.

I have been involved with the Writers' Group for over ten years, and have been very conscious of the pedagogical space, partially because of the vulnerability of some of the participants, but also because that space is a working writing community. Within the space the participants create very personal and expressive pieces based on their own life experiences, as well as highly opinionated political, cultural and social commentaries. We have no thematic or content limits, yet always operate within a safe container of respect for others and their writing.

Although no guaranteed means to accomplish this exist in an educational situation, perhaps the experience of the CMHA Writers' Group, and the general principles that govern its pedagogical space, can be helpful and evocative for other educators.

The Centrality of Playfulness

One of the subtle, but most significant principles present in the Writers' Group is the sense of acceptance and playfulness. It is a community of hospitality. When I introduce myself to a new member, I always make a point of telling her that we only have one strict rule at the Writers' Group. Inevitably there is a sigh and a deep pause while she waits for me to tell her what to do. Instead, I say that she has to have fun, and she smiles and says, "That's it? I don't have to do anything else?" "No," I tell her, "if you don't like the topic, then write about what you want. Just have fun." This principle may be perceived as being somewhat simplistic and impractical for more conventional educational settings, yet how often do educators truly welcome someone into an established learning community? In the case of the writers at CMHA Writers' Group, when a new member first becomes involved, she is usually extremely nervous, if not frightened. For one thing, she is publicly acknowledging that she is mentally ill, and is therefore extremely vulnerable. At the same time, she desires social interaction, and, perhaps hesitantly and yet hopefully, a form of personal validation and acceptance. With the simple rule of *having fun*, or to engage in *playfulness*, a new writer realizes that she can just be herself and be accepted by the other members. She is not expected to perform a role within the group, and she is allowed to explore her own ideas with dignity and respect. She can simply be.

We usually explore the ideas of others at the Writers' Group in a playful fashion. Albert often describes writing as play, and as being fun. Recently he wrote, "I personally consider writing playfulness. It must be practiced to be a good writer." In an interview, Brian Borley claimed that writing is his playground.

The idea of play and playfulness is central to the success of the Writers' Group. Nachmanovitch (1990) notes in *Freeplay: Improvisation in Life and Art*:

> Creativity exists in the searching even more than in the finding or being found. We take pleasure in energetic repetition, practice, ritual. As play, the act is its own destination.

> The focus is on process, not product. Play is intrinsically satisfying. It is not conditioned on anything else. Play, creativity, art, spontaneity, all these experiences are their own rewards and are blocked when we perform for reward or punishment, profit or loss....Play is without "why." It is self-existent. (p. 45)

As mentioned in an earlier chapter, Lensmire (1994b) suggests that teachers of writing consider Bakhtin's (1984) ideas concerning carnival as a framework for the comical, yet often profound, reexamination of social issues and conditions. The playfulness of carnival also considers the idea of *profanation*, which Bakhtin saw as "a collective, critical response to an oppressive official world" (Lensmire, 1994b, p. 381). At the Writers' Group, writers use writing in a playful manner to reexamine and reconsider personal, social, historical and cultural issues, often with powerful personal consequences. During an interview, Albert stated:

> Writers' Group has helped me a lot. It has changed me in my mind. I am a different person altogether because of it. I think differently now. I think different. I think I am a kinder person. I'm an easier person to get along with, but I haven't written all the changes that have taken place in my brain, in my head. I'm not an angry person. I'm a creative person now.

For Albert, the act of writing is a fun social activity, and the resulting written product is shared and discussed with the other members. In many ways, the Writers' Group becomes a dialogical focusing of ideas within the matrix of the individual and others. Often these discussions explore ideas that are very controversial and lively. With humor and trust, a writer is often willing to be vulnerable, and at the same time assertive and free to state his opinion, while open to listening to others' ideas.

The Importance of Conflict

Another necessary principle of the pedagogical space of the Writers' Group is the acceptance of difference and conflict within the group. In the process of meaning-making through the act of writing, individual members need to acknowledge that other members often think, feel and conceptualize ideas very differently. It is at the tension point of encountering others' ideas that individual meaning is created, in the dialogical exchange between the individual and others. Palmer (1987) mentions the importance of conflict and community in his essay "Community, Conflict, and Ways of Knowing: Ways to Deepen our Educational Agenda":

> Knowing and learning are communal acts. They require a continual cycle of discussion, disagreement and consensus over what has been and what it all means. (p. 25)

Palmer goes on to suggest that:

> A healthy community...includes conflict at its very heart, checking and correcting and enlarging the knowledge of individuals by drawing on the knowledge of the group.... Community is not opposed to conflict. On the contrary, community is precisely that place where an arena for creative conflict is protected by the compassionate fabric of human caring itself. (p. 25)

Palmer's ideas have some application in understanding the dynamics of the Writers' Group, and most educational situations. Each writer's engagement in the act of writing gives him the opportunity to explore personal perspectives on social issues. The act of writing is not simply to communicate ideas to others, which is often the most common purpose for writing in academic institutions. Instead, a writer can write for himself to construct and understand a sense of who he is as a person. At the Writers' Group, the writing that is read aloud and discussed within the pedagogical space becomes a cultural artifact that is examined as part of the complex social and cultural matrix.

The act of writing for the members of the Writers' Group is both an individual and a social process. Writing in the expressive function creates a metaphoric space of great diversity—a riparian zone—between an individual writer and others. In this space, the writer constructs a sense of self, and then negotiates relationships with others and the world through the creation of the written texts that others share in. Teachers need to create a pedagogical space that invites writers to enter their own riparian zone with confidence and respect for each other.

The Social Community and Writing

Another principle of the pedagogical space of the Writers' Group is an acknowledgment of the community, and a gentle respect for all members in the process of sharing. The writing, the reading, the sharing and the resultant discussions are all important aspects of meaning-making at the Writers' Group through dialogue and the dialectic with others. Bakhtin (1986) mentions the importance of the "responsive nature of contextual meaning. Meaning always responds to particular questions. Anything that does not respond to something seems meaningless to us; it is removed from dialogue" (p. 145). In many ways this dialectic corresponds with some of Vygotsky's (1934/1999) ideas on the nature of language:

> Thought is not merely expressed in words; it comes into existence through them. Every thought tends to connect something with something else, to establish a relation between things. Every thought moves, grows and develops, fulfills a problem. (p. 218)

At the Writers' Group, writing, which usually begins for the most part in the expressive function, develops thought and ideas through connection with others in the community, of which conflict is an integral part. Palmer (1987) writes:

> I understand community as a capacity for relatedness within individuals, relatedness not only to people, but to events in history, to nature, to the world of ideas, and yes to things of the spirit. We talk a lot in higher education about the formation of inward capacities, the capacity to tolerate ambiguity, the capacity for critical thought. I want us to talk more about those ways of knowing that form an inward capacity for relatedness. (p. 24)

The writers use the safety of the learning community found within the Writers' Group to explore serious issues—though often in a playful, creative manner, which frequently involves respectful conflict and dialogical discussion. Often these issues include controversial and "dangerous" concepts like justice, race, power and authority. Yet even in the midst of conflict and discussion there is always a deep respect and honoring of all our members.

My work with the CMHA Writers' Group does not simply demonstrate a series of pedagogical tricks or methodologies that function effectively. The work, most of all, is about *a way of being* in the world, and a way of inviting others *to be* in the world. In this sense, inviting writers to explore the riparian zone within the community of the pedagogical space is about ontology, a way of being, and allowing others to be. One member, in conversation, said that at the Writers' Group she could just be who she is, and feels that that is enough. Albert has told me that he uses the time with the group to explore who he is through his writing, and then compare that person to who he used to be. In this sense, Albert is creating a narrative of his life through the explorations of his writing and group discussions. Caroline noted in her interviews, that at the group, "there is no sympathy; there is only empathy."

At the Writers' Group, people listen and are witnesses, to each others' lives and all their experiences in the world. In so doing, the members acknowledge their successes, their failures, their progress, and their losses, and share these experiences with the other members. They learn about themselves in a meaningful and complex manner, utilizing expressive writing as a crucible. The incorporation of *lifewriting*, and personal or expressive writing in the classroom, allows individuals articulate their lives and share with others, with an acknowledgment of both gains and losses. In this sense, teachers actively encourage writers to explore issues and experiences in the riparian zone, and thereby permit them to negotiate meaning with others and the world.

What is perhaps most vital is the simple, yet fundamental, recognition of the writers as individuals, and not merely mentally ill "consumers" or "patients" as they are often labeled by the health care sector. Perhaps education has become just as blind to "students." We no longer see the student as an individual, but merely as a class member, or as a statistic in a survey, or as a number on a standardized test. Writing in the expressive function allows writers to explore their own worlds and how they relate to the larger society and culture, and recognizes this exploration as being valuable and significant.

Recognition of Diversity

The principles of playfulness, acceptance of conflict, and living in the tension that results by remaining conscious in the pedagogical space allow for the generative process of diversity. At the tension points between cooperation and conflict, and between loss and gain, meaning and true growth are facilitated. Yet many teachers and students are afraid of the tension, and perhaps even terrified by dissent and conflict. Bakhtin's (1984) concept of "carnival," as proposed by Lensmire (1994b), allows for a respectful acting out of diversity, within a pedagogical space that allows and encourages divergent thought. One simple dynamic that could change immediately in education is how students share their writing within the classroom. Although most early workshop advocates encouraged sharing, what is needed is the allowance of more critical and maverick thinking in the discussion, and a more playful negotiation of issues within the community. Perhaps by encouraging critical thinking and critical literacy, teachers can create a respectful forum for diverse thinking and ideas.

A Pedagogy of Love

To consider the question of what makes good pedagogy is an immense undertaking with no easy answers. In the context of my experiences with the Writers' Group, I would suggest that the teacher the and writers inhabit a paradoxical space—a space that allows for trust, love, care, and encouragement, yet, simultaneously and perhaps paradoxically, pushes for deeper, more critical and creative thinking. To maintain such a balance is difficult work for a teacher, but it is the heart of the practice. It is easy to swing too far to one of the binary positions and in doing so, negate the other polarity. It is necessary for a teacher to remain willing to stay in the uneasiness and uncertainty of the paradoxical space, and to do so takes enormous courage and a sense of responsibility because no easy methodologies or roadmaps exist. It is perhaps not an understatement to suggest that good teaching practice involves a pedagogy of love, with all the resultant pain and ecstasy. To teach within this pedagogical space means to be willing to dance on the lip of paradox. Yet within such a space, a writer is encouraged to go deep inside herself, value what is there, then articulate and share it with others, while at the same time negotiating meaning alongside others. In this way, a community is created that acknowledges and values self-expression, diversity, conflict, respect, and critical thinking.

Personal writing is both powerful and profound. By using the experience and observation of one's own life, the writer also engages and begins to make sense of others, the world, culture and society. The act of writing creates a metaphoric space that allows an individual to explore two directions simultaneously: both inner and outer. In the shifting flux of the exploration of the inner and outer, individuals negotiate, create, and construct meaning and understanding. Expressive writing is not simply writing about the self; rather, it is the interface to the multiplicity and diversity of the world, including other people, culture and society.

Expressive Writing as Praxis

Educators need to consciously create a pedagogical space that invites individual writers to enter the metaphorical space of the riparian zone where they can actively negotiate and integrate meaning. Moving from a theoretical base to the practicalities of classroom management and daily activities requires a shift in how we perceive the value of writing in schools. The first step is to position writing as an active, meaningful practice that involves engagement with learning, rather than a passive response to something that is happening "outside" the individual student.

Applebee (2000) noted that in the last major study of writing in secondary schools in the United States, only three percent of class work and homework involved writing original text. The majority of writing activities in school "involved writing without composing: fill in the blank and completion exercises, direct translation, or other seat work in which the text was constructed by the teacher or textbook, and the student supplied the missing information that was, typically, judged as right or wrong" (p. 1). It is therefore not difficult to see why students often perceive writing as a meaningless activity, or a waste of time.

Writing has become a passive activity in many educational situations, and often a simple way of demonstrating to the teacher that students have recognized the "correct," or prescribed answer. Teachers have also employed writing as a behavioral tool to control students by keeping them busy and quiet. In this sense, writing is not a meaningful act of engagement, and certainly not a means to explore and discover ideas and complex relationships of thought. Writing simply becomes another means of assessment, evaluation and behavioral management for an education system that often demands compliance and obedience.

I am suggesting that we utilize writing of all sorts as a central component of an active education, beginning with a repositioning of expressive, or personal, writing as a focal point of learning. Curriculum, daily teaching praxis and pedagogy need to engage and embrace individuality and diversity within a paradoxical space that includes both cooperation and conflict. Meaningful and critical writing is a key component of an active learning environment.

In early grades we allow students to choose their own topics and write about their personal experiences, but as we move into higher grades and university, the articulation of the personal is largely discouraged, denied and sometimes completely ignored. Consequently, students often don't feel any connection to the subject matter or content. Formal essays remove the "I" from the writing, and students receive constant reminders that knowledge is "out there," and that it is the writer's duty to discover it, and then represent that knowledge through the creation of text. This method of engagement often results in what Macrorie (1988) called *Engfish*, writing that sounds fine but actually says nothing. What is often missing in this type of writing is any relevant or deep understanding of the material, let alone a personal integration of this knowledge to create individual meaning.

Utilizing expressive writing, as I am suggesting, would allow a writer to explore complex social, political, cultural, and historical concepts through the filter of a personal lens of a self, even though that self is both in a state of being and an ever-shifting state of becoming. In this sense, learning and writing become meaningful acts of critical thinking and integration that acknowledge the self as a complex matrix. Expressive writing is a way of negotiating that matrix.

For instance, in secondary schools or university, it is common for a literary text to be taught as if it were an historical artifact from the distant past. The student is lead through a reading of the text to slowly reveal the meaning. Students are then asked to write essays and exams to demonstrate a knowledge and understanding of the text. Yet, as Rosenblatt (1978) has suggested in her theory of transactional reading, the relationship of reader, text, and poem (her term for the resultant meaning) is a complex matrix. Each reading is in itself a complex process, and true meaning is always negotiated between the reader and the text. Each reading will be different because each reader is different, though the text remains constant. The relationship of writer to text is equally as complex, and is in a constant state of flux. Expressive writing, when one considers the metaphor of the riparian zone, allows a writer to negotiate meaning in the matrix of the relationships, however complex.

Teachers could use expressive writing as a way of exploring complex issues. Instead of ignoring the individual student, teachers could begin with her personal perspective before leading them to a more critical approach including the ideas of others. In this way, the student has a stake in the learning and what is being covered in class. The learning is therefore not happening "out there" somewhere, but is being integrated into the student's own life. For instance, if an English teacher is using the Shakespeare text *Macbeth*, she could—instead of introducing the historical context, or the characters, or Elizabethan England—have students first do a freewrite on the topics of "evil" or "ambition" if these are themes that she is going to emphasize in the reading of the text. In this way, the individual student has a perspective and stake in the theme before entering the text of the play. Too often, students are intimidated by the language of Shakespeare, and the depth and complexity of the text. Relating the text to personal experience and the students' own lives makes the reading relevant to them, and not simply some distant, abstract, historical artifact that is meaningless to them. A teacher is not limited to having students write about abstract concepts—a student could write about personal ambition, relationships, leadership—and then later use these writings as starting points to examine the plot, themes and characters in *Macbeth*. In this way, the students have an interface and a means of intersecting meaning with *Macbeth* as a text. Studying the play then becomes a living process of understanding and growing and relating, not reading a "boring" text that is "out there" and separate from the student's own experience and life.

Utilizing personal writing as a point of engagement is not limited to literature. Teachers can use personal writing to connect students with scientific, political, or mathematical concepts. This approach would also encourage teachers to actually think about what they want students to learn, and help focus the learning process. Teachers can use this methodology and praxis in any subject because it encourages an interaction and engagement with the content itself. Even if teachers encourage students to write briefly before they begin a new concept, at the very least they would learn about the individual student's prior knowledge and personal interest.

Students could use the lens of the personal to explore almost any subject or idea. Instead of ignoring the personal, modern curriculum design could reposition expressive writing as a central component of all learning. Of course, that does not mean simply ending with various forms of personal writing. A student still needs to write in a great variety of function categories. I am simply suggesting that we consider a student's stake in her own learning, and not negate her individual experience, especially as she moves up the hierarchy of higher education. Positioning the student as the focus of any learning experience is of course not a new idea. What I am suggesting is a simple, practical means of validating a student's own thoughts and ideas as articulated through expressive writing as the interface to engage in all learning, no matter how abstract and conceptual.

Historical and social concepts or issues can be addressed in a similar manner. A teacher could have the students respond to the concept or issue from a personal point of view first. This preliminary act of writing immediately engages the students, and encourages them to think about the issue, and become active learners. Of course, it is important to note that teachers must not stop with the students' first thoughts, which are often superficial. The students could share their writing and discuss it openly to allow for the open examination of ideas in a safe pedagogical space, which permits and encourages conflict, critical thinking, and the embracing of diversity and difference. The teacher could then introduce concepts in a forum that is active, not passive. Students would be encouraged to go beyond their own limited views and perceptions to enter an active pedagogical space that allows for individual and diverse expression. Within that space, students writing in the expressive function must clearly articulate and express their ideas to others.

At this point, other forms of writing can be demonstrated, not as forms that negate the perspective of the individual, but rather as genres that more effectively communicate ideas to others. Britton's (1970, 1975) suggestion that expressive writing is the matrix of all forms of writing has been largely misinterpreted and simplified. There is nothing natural about moving from the expressive function to transactional and poetic forms of writing. All writing structures are constructed and socially negotiated. Expressive writing simply allows writers to access their ideas more readily at first; however, writing has a myriad of genres and structures, and need not stop with exclusively personal or expressive forms. Formal essay structures need to be taught as means to clearly articulate ideas to others. What really is shifting, in pedagogical terms, is the focus on the individual as a validated and central component of any learning situation.

Kamler (2001) has suggested that educators use "story rather than voice as a metaphor of the personal" (p. 176). This conceptualization of a story as a narrative construction "allows for a more textual orientation than voice, a closer attention to text and textuality, a different treatment of the person (who writes) and the personal (the text they write)" (p. 177). This shift in focus allows for a distancing effect, and enables a teacher to use the resultant text as an artifact that can be explored and examined independent of the writer. In many ways this is exactly what occurs at the Writers' Group when writing is read aloud, shared, and examined as text. Yet at the same time, the writer is not negated and invisible. Writing in the expressive function is a means of conceptualizing and validating the narrative of the individual, as well as a way of processing and negotiating the complex relationships that form our way of being in the world.

If we consider narrative as a way of knowing (Bruner, 1986), as well as a conceptual structure that is often literary in nature which evokes that knowing, and finally as a way of being in the world, it is possible to see the complexity of what it means to write in the expressive function. By repositioning expressive writing as a central activity in education, we are accessing learning from a narrative way of knowing, which augments and supplements paradigmatic knowing. In this sense we enfold rational, linear, sequential ways of thought, within a relational way of knowing. Utilizing expressive writing allows us to access the narrative ways of knowing and to engage paradigmatic ways of knowing from a personal point of view, always taking into account the relationship of others, as well as social and cultural forces. Writing in the expressive function is always about writing at the edge.

Coda

There is a light covering of snow on the ground. I stand by my car and look at the moon rising through clouds. I walk past David's bike, locked to a support beam of the entrance to CMHA, and enter the building.

I sit at one of the long tables. I spread out several note pads on the tabletop, and hundreds of pages of loose-leaf, my field notes merging into creative work, all becoming a field of intertextuality.

I'm a little early, and not all the members have arrived yet. Brian and Joe have already set up the tables, and Joe has already made the coffee.

Joe sits down across from me with a cup of coffee. "Sorry to hear about your Mom," he says. He keeps his eyes on the table and doesn't look up at me.

"Thanks," I say.

Brian comes into the room from the kitchen. "Did you get my e-mail?" he asks.

"Yes, thank you."

Fiona hands me a card. "It's for your aunt. It just says, 'with my deepest sympathy.' Is that okay?"

"It's fine. She'll really appreciate it."

"We missed you last week," Ann says.

"Sorry, I was writing the eulogy."

"We know how busy you've been."

Fiona slides another card across the table top for the other members to sign. "This one is for you," she says.

David has been standing at the back wall reading notices. He sits down, takes some paper out of his back pocket and spreads it on the table. He takes off his jacket and drapes it over the back of his chair. "Have we started yet? Have we got a topic?"

"Not yet," I say.

Graham arrives. He hasn't been here for a few weeks. He has a binder with a torn black paper cover with all his writing in it. The binder looks like it is about to burst, which is also how Graham tends to write. Everything pours out of him, and he can't write fast enough to collect it all. He now tends to write fragments of longer pieces, which he doesn't always finish. He spreads out paper in front of him. Lately he's been using loose-leaf which he keeps adding to the binder.

Donna sits quietly. She's having a hard time. She gets bored and sometimes stares into space seemingly disassociated from everything around her. Someone puts a cup of water in front of her. She just nods.

There are now nine writers here. Ten actually, since I am one of the group. I have the others leave a space for Warren and Albert who are usually fifteen minutes late. We're all sitting around the tables now, many with coffee, all with pen and paper. I ask how everyone has been, and we start talking about their weeks, and about day-to-day experiences.

I try to give everyone a chance to talk, but at the same time keep the discussion quite brief. It is usually a balancing act. A few months ago, one of the writers complained that we had been talking too much at the last few meetings. "This isn't a debating club," she had said. The obvious solution would be to focus on the act of writing. This is the Writers' Group after all, but the situation is complex. I have always tried to provide an opportunity for each member to speak and to be heard. Many of these people have simply been discarded and forgotten by the rest of society. I think it is important that they have a voice, and I have worked hard at providing a place where they can speak openly. Now, Ann was suggesting that I had perhaps been too successful. We were now talking too much. Instead of making an autocratic decision to cut the discussion, I asked the group what they thought. What followed, of course, was a discussion about talking and writing. This may have been somewhat ironic, talking about too much talking, but it provided a valuable forum for the writers on a number of levels. The group members always decide what they want to do. Issues of power and choice are usually left to the writers. Although I could be seen as being in a position of power, the power is an illusion for several reasons. For instance, if I were to focus on errors and mistakes and the weaknesses of the members' writing, their responses and efforts would be entirely different. More importantly, if the group did not like what I was doing, they simply would not attend. In actuality I have only the power they give me. Ultimately, they always have choice.

A woman enters from the office area. I've never seen her before.

"Hi," I say.

"Is this the Writers' Group?" she asks.

"You're at the right place," says Jane.

"Let's make some space for...what's your name?" I ask.

"Jennifer." Her voice is nearly a whisper.

"For Jennifer. How about at the end there? Is that okay? Do you have paper and a pen?" I ask.

"No."

"I've got an extra pen she can borrow," says Jane.

Fiona rips out a couple of pages from her notebook. "She can have this," she says.

"Do you know anyone here?" I ask.

"No," she says.

"Why don't we introduce ourselves to Jennifer?"

We go around the room, briefly introducing ourselves. When we get to Brian, after he has introduced himself, he says, "We've been doing this for years. Maybe you should tell her what we do, and the rules."

"Okay. We basically write, and then take turns reading what we write aloud."

Jennifer looks up. Her eyes open wide, but she doesn't say anything.

"But you don't have to do that if you don't want to."

"And if you think Jeff's topics are stupid, you can always write what you want," says Ann.

"Anything?" Jennifer asks.

"That's right. I just give you some ideas. But I do want you to know that we have one very serious rule here."

"What's that?"

"You have to have fun." The rest of the group laughs. "Yes, you have to have some fun."

"Really?" Jennifer asks. "Just have fun? I'll try."

There is a noise at the front door, and Warren and Albert arrive, right on time fifteen minutes late. Warren leads the way, and shuffles to a chair. "Sorry, sorry. What's the topic?" He gets out a notebook from his pocket.

"We haven't started yet," I say.

"Not yet? Then you're late," says Warren.

Albert sits across from me. He doesn't say a word. He just smiles as he sits down. Then he stands up and goes to borrow some paper and a pen from someone. When he sits down again he says, "What are we doing?"

"Introducing ourselves," I say.

"Oh," says Albert. "I'm Albert. I was the first member of the writing group. What's your name?"

"Jennifer."

"What's the topic?" says Albert. "Nobody told me."

"Did you hear about those two police officers?" says Graham.

"You mean the charges against them?" says David.

"What do they want now?" says Brian.

"There is no justice," says Albert.

"Only the rich have justice."

"Remember when I told you that we had to talk to that constable?" says Warren.

"Why are we talking?" says Ann.

"It's sometimes good to talk," says Brian. "I like hearing what other people think."

"But can't we talk after we write?" says Janet.

"Can we get writing? We're talking too much. This is a writing group," says Ann.

"Okay. Fair enough. Any ideas?" I say. "Do you want to write about the police?"

"No, I'm tired of thinking about them," says Donna.

"Anything else? I can't think tonight," I say.

"You're a man. What do you know?" says Caroline.

I laugh. "You're right. Here's another idea. What if we write about talking and writing?"

"Very funny," says Ann.

"We could write about the relationship between the two. Do you need to talk to be able to write?" I ask.

"Can we get started? I need to catch a bus."

"Then, let's get started. You have ten minutes," I say.

"Fifteen," says David.

"Fine. Fifteen. Let's get started."

And we do. We begin writing. All of us, even Jennifer. There is no talking. There is no sound in the room except the scuffling of pens on paper, and the breathing of the writers. Breath and paper. We write. We do not hesitate. We write at the edge. We write as if our lives depend on it.

References

Allen, G. (2000). Language, power, and the consciousness: A writing experiment at the University of Toronto. In *Writing and healing: Toward an informed practice*, eds. C. M. Anderson and M. M. MacCurdy, (pp. 249-290). Urbana, IL: National Council of Teachers of English.

Alvermann, D.E., & Hruby, G.G. (2003). Fictive representation: An alternative method for reporting research. In J. Flood & D. Lapp & J. Squire & J. Jensen (Eds.), *Handbook of research on teaching the English language arts* (pp. 260-272). Mahwah, NJ: Lawrence Erlbaum Associates.

Applebee, A. (2000). Alternative models of writing development. In *Perspectives on writing: Research/theory/practice*. Newark, DE: International Reading Association, via http://cela.albany.edu/publication/article/writing.htm.

Atwell, N. (1987). *In the middle: Writing, reading and learning with adolescents.* Portsmouth, NH: Boynton/Cook Publishers.

Atwell, N. (1990). *Coming to know: Writing to learn in the intermediate grades.* Portsmouth, NH; Toronto, ON: Heinemann; Irwin Pub.

Bakhtin, M. M. (1981). *The dialogic imagination: Four essays*, trans. C. H. Emerson, ed. Michael Holquist. Austin, TX: University of Texas Press.

Bakhtin, M. M. (1984). *Rabelais and his world*, trans. H. Iswolsky. Bloomington, IN: Indiana University Press.

Bakhtin, M. M. (1986). *Speech genres and other late essays*, eds. C. H. Emerson and Michael Holquist. Austin, TX: University of Texas Press.

Bakhtin, M. M. (1994). *The Bakhtin reader: Selected writings of Bakhtin, Medvedev, Voloshinov*, ed. Pam Morris. London: Edward Arnold.

Barone, T. E. (1990). Using the narrative text as an occasion for conspiracy. In *Qualitative inquiry in education: The continuing debate*, eds. E. W. Eisner & A. Peshkin, (pp. 305-326). New York: Teachers College Press.

Barone, T., Carey, C., Crissman, C., Dunlop, R., Eisner, E., & Gardner, H. (1999). *Shaking the ivory tower: Writing, advising, and critiquing the postmodern dissertation.* Paper presented at the American Educational Research Association: On the threshold of the twenty-first century, Montreal.

Barone, T., & Eisner, E. (1997). Arts-based educational research. In *Complementary methods for research in education*, ed. R. M. Jaeger, (2nd ed., pp. 73-99). Washington, DC: American Educational Research Association.

Bartholomae, D. (1995). Writing with teachers: A conversation with Peter Elbow. *College Composition and Communication, 46*(1), 62-71.

Bartholomae, D., & Elbow, P. (1995). Interchanges: Responses to Bartholomae and Elbow. *College Composition and Communication, 46*(1), 84-92.

Bentley, R., & Butler, S. (1986). Lifewriting: Self-exploration through writing. *BCETA Journal, 87*, 21-24.

Bentley, R., & Butler, S. (1988). *Lifewriting: Self-exploration and life review through writing—a text for teachers, instructors of writing, and community leaders.* Dubuque, IA: Kendall/Hunt Publishing Co.

Berlin, J. (1987). *Rhetoric and reality: Writing instruction in American colleges, 1900-1985.* Carbondale, IL: Southern Illinois University Press.

Berlin, J. (1988). Rhetoric and ideology in the writing class. *College English, 50*(5), 477-494.

Berlin, J. (1990). Writing instruction in school and college English, 1890-1985. In *A short history of writing instruction: From ancient Greece to twentieth-century America*, ed. J. Murphy. Davis, CA: Hermagoras Press.

Bizzell, P. (1992). Cognition, convention, and certainty. What we need to know about writing, *Academic discourse and critical consciousness* (pp. 75-104). Pittsburgh, PA: University of Pittsburgh Press.

Blake, B. E. (1995). Broken silences: Writing and the construction of "Cultural Texts" by urban, preadolescent girls. *Journal of Educational Thought, 29*(2), 163-180.

Bohm, D. (1980). *Wholeness and the implicate order.* London; Boston: Routledge & Kegan Paul.

Bohm, D., & Peat, F. D. (2000). *Science, order, and creativity* (2nd ed.). London: Routledge.

Borley, B. (2000). *Sarah Tallhorse.* Unpublished novel.

Britton, J. (1970/1985). *Language and learning: The importance of speech in children's development.* Harmondsworth, Middlesex: Penguin.

Britton, J. (1972). Writing to learn and learning to write. In *Prospect and retrospect: Selected essays of James Britton*, ed. G. M. Pradl, (pp. 94-111). Upper Montclair, NJ: Boynton/Cook.

Britton, J. (1979). Notes on a working hypothesis about writing. In *Prospect and retrospect: Selected essays of James Britton*, ed. G. M. Pradl, (pp. 123-138). Upper Montclair, NJ: Boynton/Cook.

Britton, J. (1980). Shaping at the point of utterance. In *Prospect and retrospect: Selected essays of James Britton*, ed. G. M. Pradl, (pp. 139-145). Upper Montclair, NJ: Boynton/Cook.

Britton, J. (1982). English teaching: Retrospect and prospect. In *Prospect and retrospect: Selected essays of James Britton*, ed. G. M. Pradl, (pp. 201-215). Upper Montclair, NJ: Boynton/Cook.

Britton, J., Burgess, T., Martin, N., McLeod, A., & Rosen, H. (1975). *The development of writing abilities (11-18)*. London: Macmillian Education.

Brotchie, A. (1995). *Surrealist games*, ed. Mel Gooding. London: Redstone Press.

Bruner, J. S. (1986). *Actual minds, possible worlds*. Cambridge, MA: Harvard University Press.

Bruner, J. S. (1987). Life as narrative. *Social Research*, 54(1), 11-32.

Bruner, J. S. (1988). Research currents: Life as narrative. *Language Arts*, 65(6), 574-583.

Bruner, J. S. (1990). *Acts of meaning*. Cambridge, MA: Harvard University Press.

Bruner, J. (1996). *The culture of education*. Cambridge, MA: Harvard University Press.

Bruner, J., & Weisser, S. (1991). The invention of self: Autobiography and its forms. In *Literacy and orality*, eds. D. Olson & N. Torrance. Cambridge, MA: Cambridge University Press.

Buford, B. (1996, June 24). The seductions of storytelling. *The New Yorker*, 11-12.

Butler, S. (1985). Writing for posterity. *Adult Education*, 58(3), 234-240.

Butler, S. (Ed.). (1999). *Beginnings: Lifewriting from Brock House*. Vancouver, BC: Brock House Writers.

Butler, S. J., & Bentley, T. R. (1990). *Lifewriting: Literacy and self-awareness through autobiographical writing*, (Eric Document Reproduction Service No. ED315777).

Butler, S., & Bentley, R. (1992). Literacy through lifewriting. *English Quarterly*, 24(3), 33-41.

Butler, S., & Bentley, R. (1997). *Lifewriting: Learning through personal narrative*. Scarborough, ON: Pippin Publishing.

Butler, S. J., & Mansfield, E. A. (1995). Lifewriting in a secondary school. *English Quarterly*, 28(1), 12-17.

Calkins, L. M. (1983). *Lessons from a child: On the teaching and learning of writing.* Exeter, NH: Heinemann Educational Books.

Calkins, L. M. (1986). *The art of teaching writing.* Portsmouth, NH: Heinemann.

Calkins, L. M. (with Harwayne, S.). (1991). *Living between the lines.* Portsmouth, NH; Toronto, ON: Heinemann; Irwin Pub.

Calkins, L. M., & Stratton, P. (1994). *The art of teaching writing.* Portsmouth, NH; Toronto, ON: Heinemann; Irwin.

Cameron, W. B. (1950/1926). *Blood red the sun* (Rev. ed.). Calgary, AB: Kenway Pub. Co.

Charters, A. (Ed.). (1992). *The portable beat reader.* New York: Penguin Books.

Chatsis, A. (in progress). *Horsechild.* Unpublished novel.

Clandinin, D. J., & Connelly, F. M. (1996). Teachers' professional knowledge landscapes: Teacher stories-stories of teachers-school stories-stories of schools. *Educational Reseacher, 25*(3), 24–30.

Clandinin, D. J., & Connelly, M. F. (2000). *Narrative inquiry: Experience and story in qualitative research.* San Francisco, CA: Jossey-Baas Publishers.

Coles, W. E. (1988). *The plural I and after.* Portsmouth, NH: Boynton/Cook Publishers.

Connelly, F. M., & Clandinin, D. J. (1990). Stories of experience and narrative inquiry. *Educational Researcher, 19*(5), 2–14.

Cope, B., & Kalantzis, M. (1993). *The powers of literacy: A genre approach to teaching writing.* Pittsburgh, PA: University of Pittsburgh Press.

Cranny-Francis, A., & Martin, J. R. (1993, September). Making new meanings: Literacy and linguistic perspectives on the function of genre in textual practice. *English in Australia 105,* 30–43.

Csikszentmihalyi, M. (1990). *Flow: The psychology of optimal experience.* New York: HarperPerennial.

Csikszentmihalyi, M. (1993). *The evolving self: A psychology for the third millennium.* New York: HarperPerennial.

Csikszentmihalyi, M. (1997). *Finding flow: The psychology of engagement with everyday life.* New York: Basic Books.

Csikszentmihalyi, M. (1997b). *Creativity: Flow and the psychology of discovery and invention.* New York: HarperPerennial.

Delpit, L. (1988). The silenced dialogue: Power and pedagogy in educating other people's children. *Harvard Educational Review, 58*(3), 280–298.

Delpit, L. (1995). *Other people's children: Cultural conflict in the classroom.* New York: The New Press.

Denzin, N. K. (1997). *Interpretive ethnography: Ethnographic practices for the 21st century.* Thousand Oaks, CA: Sage.

References

Diversi, M. (1998). Glimpses of street life: Representing lived experience through short stories. *Qualitative Inquiry, 4*(2), 131–147.

Dixon, J. (1975). *Growth through English: Set in the perspective of the seventies* (3rd ed.). London: Oxford University Press for the National Association for the Teaching of English.

Dreher, B. (1980). Directing a writing program for retirees. *English Journal, 69*(7), 54–56.

Eisner, E. (1997). The promise and perils of alternative forms of data representation. *Educational Researcher, 26*(6), 4–11.

Elbow, P. (1973/1998). *Writing without teachers* (2nd ed.). New York: Oxford University Press.

Elbow, P. (1981). *Writing with power: Techniques for mastering the writing process.* New York: Oxford University Press.

Elbow, P. (1995). Being a writer vs. being an academic: A conflict in goals. *College Composition and Communication, 46*(1), 72–83.

Elbow, P. (1998). *Writing without teachers* (2nd ed.). New York: Oxford University Press.

Elbow, P. (2000). *Everyone can write: Essays toward a hopeful theory of writing and teaching writing.* New York: Oxford University Press.

Ellis, C. (1997). Evocative autoethnography: Writing emotionally about our lives. In *Representation and the text: Re-framing the narrative voice*, eds. W. Tierney & Y. Lincoln, (pp. 115–139). Albany, NY: State University of New York Press.

Ellis, C., & Bochner, A. P. (2000). Autoethnography, personal narrative, reflexivity: Research as subject. In *Handbook of qualitative research*, eds. N. K. Denzin & Y. S. Lincoln, (pp. 733–768). Thousand Oaks, CA: Sage.

Ellis, C., & Flaherty, M. G. (Eds.). (1992). *Investigating subjectivity: Research on lived experience.* Newbury Park, CA: Sage.

Emig, J. (1971). *The composing processes of twelfth graders. Research Report no. 13.* Urbana, IL: National Council of Teachers of English.

Faigley, L. (1986). Competing theories of process: A critique and a proposal. *College English, 48*(6), 527–542.

Faigley, L. (1992). *Fragments of rationality: Postmodernity and the subject of composition.* Pittsburgh, PA: University of Pittsburgh Press.

Fine, M. (1987). Silencing in public schools. *Language Arts, 64*(2), 157–174.

Fish, S. (1980). Interpreting the variorum. In *Reader-response criticism: From formalism to post-structuralism*, ed. J. P. Tompkins, (pp. 164–184). Baltimore, MD: Johns Hopkins University Press.

Flower, L., & Hayes, J. R. (1981). A cognitive process theory of writing. *College Composition and Communication, 32,* 365-387.

Foucault, M. (1988). Technologies of the self. In *Technologies of the self: A seminar with Michel Foucault,* eds. L. H. Martin, H. Gutman and P. H. Hutton, (pp. 17-49). Amherst, MA: University of Massachusetts Press.

Foucault, M. (1997). *Ethics: Subjectivity and truth* (Vol. 1), trans. R. Hurley, ed. P. Rabinow. New York: New Press.

Freedman, A., & Medway, P. (Eds.). (1994a). *Genre and the new rhetoric.* London; Bristol, PA: Taylor & Francis.

Freedman, A., & Medway, P. (Eds.). (1994b). *Learning and teaching genre.* Portsmouth, MH: Boynton/Cook Publishers.

Freire, P. (1985). Reading the world and reading the word: An interview with Paulo Freire. *Language Arts, 62*(1), 15-21.

Freire, P. (with notes by Freire, A. M. A.). (1994). *Pedagogy of hope: Reliving pedagogy of the oppressed.* New York: Continuum.

Freire, P. (1995). *Pedagogy of the oppressed* (New revised 20th-anniversary ed.). New York: Continuum.

Freire, P., & Macedo, D. (1987). *Literacy: Reading the word and the world.* South Hadley, MA: Bergin and Garvey.

Fuentes, C. (1985). *The old gringo.* New York: Farrar Straus Giroux.

Fulford, R. (1999). *The triumph of narrative: Storytelling in the age of mass culture.* Toronto, ON: Anansi.

Geertz, C. (1973). *The interpretation of cultures.* New York: Basic Books.

Gere, A. R. (1987). *Writing groups: History, theory, and implications.* Carbondale, IL: Southern Illinois University Press.

Gillis, C., & Wagner, L. (1980). *Life-Writing: Writing workshops and outreach procedures.* Paper presented at the American Educational Research Association, Boston, MA, (Eric Document Reproduction Service No. ED186824).

Giroux, H. (1987). Introduction. In *Literacy: Reading the word and the world,* eds. P. Freire & D. Macedo, (pp. 1-27). Westport, CT: Bergin and Garvey.

Giroux, H. A. (1997). *Pedagogy and the politics of hope: Theory, culture, and schooling: A critical reader.* Boulder, CO: Westview Press.

Goffman, E. (1959). *The presentation of self in everyday life.* New York: Anchor Books.

Graves, D. H. (1973). *Children's writing: Research directions and hypotheses based upon an examination of the writing processes of seven year old children.* Unpublished Ed.D. dissertation, State University of New York at Buffalo, Buffalo, NY.

Graves, D. H. (1975). An examination of the writing processes of seven year old children. *Research in the Teaching of English, 9,* 227-241.

Graves, D. H. (1983). *Writing: Teachers and children at work.* Exeter, UK: Heinemann Educational Books.

Graves, D. H. (1994). *A fresh look at writing.* Portsmouth, NH; Toronto, ON: Heinemann; Irwin Pub.

Hairston, M. (1982). The winds of change: Thomas Kuhn and the revolution in the teaching of writing. *College Composition and Communication, 33*(1), 76-88.

Harding, D. W. (1937). The role of the onlooker. *Scrutiny, 6*(3), 247-258.

Hemley, R. (1994). *Turning life into fiction.* Cincinnati, OH: Story Press.

Holbrook, D. (1964). *English for the rejected: Training literacy in the lower streams of the secondary school.* Cambridge, UK: Cambridge University Press.

Holbrook, D. (1967). *English for maturity* (2nd ed.). London: Cambridge University Press.

Holbrook, D. (1979). *English for meaning.* Windsor, UK; Atlantic Highlands, NJ: Humanities Press.

Holstein, J., & Gubrium, J. (1995). *The active interview.* Thousand Oaks, CA: Sage Publications.

Holstein, J., & Gubrium, J. (1997). Active interviewing. In *Qualitative research: Theory, method and practice,* ed. D. Silverman, (pp. 113-129). Thousand Oaks, CA: Sage Publications.

hooks, b. (1999). *Remembered rapture: The writer at work.* New York: Henry Holt.

Jay, M. (1993). *Downcast eyes: The denigration of vision in twentieth-century French thought.* Berkeley, CA: University of California Press.

Kamler, B. (2001). *Relocating the personal: A critical writing pedagogy.* Albany, NY: State University of New York Press.

Kincheloe, J. (1991). *Teachers as researchers: Qualitative inquiry as a path to empowerment.* London: Falmer.

Kinneavy, J. L. (1971). *A theory of discourse.* Englewood Cliffs, NJ: Prentice-Hall.

Koch, K. (1977). *I never told anybody: Teaching poetry writing in a nursing home.* New York: Random House.

Kress, G. R. (1997). *Before writing: Rethinking the paths to literacy.* London, UK; New York: Routledge.

Kuhn, T. S. (1962). *The structure of scientific revolutions.* Chicago, IL: University of Chicago Press.

Lee, D. (2002). Body music: Notes on rhythm in poetry. In T. Lilburn (Ed.), *Thinking and singing: Poetry and the practice of philosophy.* Toronto, ON: Cormorant Books.

Leggo, C. (1989). *Search(ing) (for) voices(s).* Unpublished Ph.D. dissertation, University of Alberta, Edmonton, AB.

Lensmire, T. J. (1994a). *When children write: Critical re-visions of the writing workshop.* New York: Teachers College Press.

Lensmire, T. (1994b). Writing workshop as carnival: Reflections on an alternative learning environment. *Harvard Educational Review,* 64(4), 371–391.

Lensmire, T. (1997). The teacher as Dostoevskian novelist. *Research in the Teaching of English,* 31(3), 367–392.

Lensmire, T. (1998). Rewriting student voice. *Journal of Curriculum Studies,* 30(3), 261–291.

Lensmire, T. J. (2000). *Powerful writing, responsible teaching.* New York: Teachers College Press.

Lincoln, Y. S. (1995). Emerging criteria for quality in qualitative and interpretive research. *Qualitative Inquiry,* 1(3), 275–289.

Lincoln, Y. S., & Guba, E. G. (1985). *Naturalistic inquiry.* Beverly Hills, CA: Sage Publications.

Macrorie, K. (1970). *Telling writing.* New York: Hayden Book Co.

Macrorie, K. (1974). *A vulnerable teacher.* Rochelle Park, NJ: Hayden Book Company.

Macrorie, K. (1976). *Writing to be read* (Rev. 2nd ed.). Rochelle Park, NJ: Hayden Book Co.

Macrorie, K. (1980). *Searching writing: A contextbook.* Rochelle Park, NJ: Hayden Book Company.

Macrorie, K. (1988). *The I-search paper: Revised edition of searching writing.* Portsmouth, NH: Boynton/Cook Publishers.

McAdams, D. P. (1996). *The stories we live by: Personal myths and the making of the self.* New York: Guilford Press.

Merriam, S. B. (1998). *Qualitative research and case study applications in education: Revised and expanded from case study research in education.* San Francisco, CA: Jossey-Bass Publishers.

Miller, J. P., & Seller, W. (1985). *Curriculum: perspectives and practice.* New York: Longman.

Miller, J. R. (1996). *Big Bear (Mistahimusqua).* Toronto, ON: ECW Press.

Minock, M. (1994). The bad marriage: A revisionist view of James Britton's expressive-writing hypothesis in American practice. In *Taking stock: The writing process movement in the '90s,* eds. L. Tobin & T. Newkirk, (pp. 153–175). Portsmouth, NH: Boynton/Cook.

Moffett, J. (1968). *Teaching the universe of discourse.* Boston, MA: Houghton Mifflin.

Moffett, J. (1973). *A student-centered language arts curriculum, grades K–13: A handbook for teachers.* Boston, MA: Houghton Mifflin.

Murphy, C. (2000). *The haunted eyes.* unpublished novel.
Murray, D. M. (1968). *A writer teaches writing: A practical method of teaching composition.* Boston, MA: Houghton Mifflin.
Murray, D. M. (1984). *Write to learn.* New York: Holt Rinehart and Winston.
Murray, D. M. (1985). *A Writer teaches writing* (2nd ed.). Boston, MA: Houghton Mifflin Co.
Murray, D. M. (1991). All writing is autobiography. *College Composition and Communication, 42*(1), 66-74.
Murray, D. M. (1999). *Write to learn* (6th ed.). New York: Harcourt Brace.
Nachmanovitch, S. (1990). *Free play: Improvisation in life and art.* New York: G. P. Putnam's Sons.
Newkirk, T. (1997). *The performance of self in student writing.* Portsmouth, NH: Boynton/Cook Publishers: Heinemann.
Nye, E. (2000). The more I tell my story: Writing as healing in an HIV/AIDS community. In *Writing and healing: Toward an informed practice*, eds. C. M. Anderson & M. M. MacCurdy, (pp. 385-415). Urbana, IL: National Council of Teachers of English.
Ong, W. J. (1982). *Orality and literacy: The technologizing of the word.* London; New York: Methuen.
Painter, C., & Martin, J. R. (1985, May). *Writing to mean: Teaching genres across the curriculum.* Paper presented at the Writing to Mean Conference, University of Sydney.
Palmer, P. J. (1987). Community, conflict, and ways of knowing: Ways to deepen our educational agenda. *Change 19*(5), 20-25.
Perry, P. H. (2000). *A composition of consciousness: Roads of reflection from Freire and Elbow.* New York: Peter Lang Publishing.
Picasso, P. (1972). *Picasso on art: A selection of views.* New York: Viking Press.
Polkinghorne, D. (1988). *Narrative knowing and the human sciences.* Albany, NY: State University of New York Press.
Richardson, L. (1990). *Writing strategies: Reaching diverse audiences* (Vol. 21). Newbury Park, CA: Sage Publications.
Richardson, L. (2000). Writing: A method of inquiry. In *Handbook of qualitative research*, eds. N. K. Denzin & Y. S. Lincoln, (2nd ed., pp. 923-948). Thousand Oaks. CA: Sage.
Ricoeur, P. (1984). *Time and narrative.* Chicago, IL: University of Chicago Press.
Ricoeur, P. (1998). The hermeneutical function of distantiation. In *Art and interpretation: An anthology of readings in aesthetics and the philosophy of art*, ed. E. Dayton, (pp. 363-371). Peterborough, ON; Orchard Park, NY: Broadview Press.

Rilke, R. M. (1999). *The essential Rilke: Selected and translated by Galway Kinnell and Hannah Liebmann*. New York: Ecco Press.

Rodman, S. (1957). *Conversations with artists*. New York: Capricorn Books.

Rohman, D. G. (1965). Pre-Writing: The stage of discovery in the writing process. *College Composition and Communication, 16*, 106–112.

Romano, T. (1987). *Clearing the way: Working with teenage writers*. Portsmouth, NH: Heinemann.

Rorty, R. (1979). *Philosophy and the mirror of nature*. Princeton, NJ: Princeton University Press.

Rosen, H. (1987). *Stories and meanings*. Sheffield, UK: National Association for the Teaching of English.

Rosenblatt, L. (1978). *The reader, the text, the poem: The transactional theory of the literary work*. Carbondale, IL: Southern Illinois University.

Rosenblatt, L. M. (1988). *Writing and reading: The transactional theory. Technical report No. 416*. Champaign, IL: University of Illinois at Urbana-Champaign.

Sconiers, Z. D., & Rosiek, J. L. (2000). Voices inside schools: Historical perspective as an important element of teachers' knowledge: A sonata-form case study of equity issues in a chemistry classroom. *Harvard Educational Review, 70*(3), 370–404.

Seidman, I. (1998). *Interviewing as qualitative research: A guide for researchers in education and the social sciences* (2nd ed.). New York: Teachers College Press.

Shafer, G. (2001). Composition and a prison community of writers. *English Journal, 90*(5), 75–81.

Sluyter, D. (2001). *The Zen commandments: Ten suggestions for a life of inner freedom*. New York: Jeremy P. Tarcher/Putnam.

Staples, K. (1981). *A writing course for elders: Outreach, growth, synthesis*. Paper presented at the Community College Humanities Association Conference, Farmer's Branch, TX, (Eric Document Reproduction Service No. ED212335).

Swales, J. (1990). *Genre analysis: English in academic and research settings*. Cambridge, UK; New York: Cambridge University Press.

Tobin, L., & Newkirk, T. (Eds.). (1994). *Taking stock: The writing process movement in the '90s*. Portsmouth, NH: Boynton/Cook.

Tompkins, G. E. (2000). *Teaching writing: Balancing process and product* (3rd ed.). Upper Saddle River, NJ: Prentice-Hall Inc.

Turkle, S. (1995). *Life on the screen: Identity in the age of the Internet*. New York: Touchstone.

Turner, M. (1996). *The literary mind*. Oxford, UK: Oxford University Press.

References

Tyler, S. (1986). Post-modern ethnography: From document of the occult to occult document. In *Writing culture: The poetics and politics of ethnography*, eds. J. Clifford & G. E. Marcus, (pp. 122-140). Berkeley, CA: University of California Press.

Yagelski, R. P. (1994). Who's afraid of subjectivity? The composing process and postmodernism or A student of Donald Murray enters the age of postmodernism. In *Taking stock: The writing process movement in the '90s*, eds. L. Tobin & T. Newkirk, (pp. 203-217). Portsmouth, NH: Boynton/Cook.

Vanderhaeghe, G. (1982). *Man descending: Selected stories.* Toronto, ON: Macmillan.

Vanderhaeghe, G. (1996). *The Englishman's boy.* Toronto, ON: McClelland & Stewart.

Vanderhaeghe, G. (2002). *The last crossing.* Toronto, ON: McClelland & Stewart.

Vygotsky, L. S. (1930/1978). *Mind in society: The development of higher psychological processes.* Cambridge, MA: Harvard University Press.

Vygotsky, L. S. (1934/1999). *Thought and language* (Rev. ed.). Cambridge, MA: MIT Press.

White, D. R., & Hellerich, G. (1998). *Labyrinths of the mind: The self in the postmodern age.* Albany, NY: State University of New York Press.

Willinsky, J. (1990). *The new literacy: Redefining reading and writing in the schools.* New York: Routledge.

Witherell, C., & Noddings, N. (Eds.). (1991). *Stories lives tell: Narratives and dialogue in education.* New York: Teachers College Press.

COUNTERPOINTS

Studies in the Postmodern Theory of Education

General Editors
Joe L. Kincheloe & Shirley R. Steinberg

Counterpoints publishes the most compelling and imaginative books being written in education today. Grounded on the theoretical advances in criticalism, feminism, and postmodernism in the last two decades of the twentieth century, Counterpoints engages the meaning of these innovations in various forms of educational expression. Committed to the proposition that theoretical literature should be accessible to a variety of audiences, the series insists that its authors avoid esoteric and jargonistic languages that transform educational scholarship into an elite discourse for the initiated. Scholarly work matters only to the degree it affects consciousness and practice at multiple sites. Counterpoints' editorial policy is based on these principles and the ability of scholars to break new ground, to open new conversations, to go where educators have never gone before.

For additional information about this series or for the submission of manuscripts, please contact:
>Joe L. Kincheloe & Shirley R. Steinberg
>c/o Peter Lang Publishing, Inc.
>275 Seventh Avenue, 28th floor
>New York, New York 10001

To order other books in this series, please contact our Customer Service Department:
>(800) 770-LANG (within the U.S.)
>(212) 647-7706 (outside the U.S.)
>(212) 647-7707 FAX

Or browse online by series:
>www.peterlangusa.com